THE LITTLE BOOK OF CHURCH LEADERSHIP

A LITTLE BOOK WITH BIG IDEAS

KEVIN SIMINGTON

Copyright © 2020 by Kevin Simington

All rights reserved.

No part of this book may be reproduced in any form or by any electronic or mechanical means, including information storage and retrieval systems, without written permission from the author, except for the use of brief quotations in a book review.

Unless otherwise specified, Scripture quotations are from the New International Version Bible, copyright © 1973, 1978, 1984, 2011, Zondervan, Grand Rapids, Michigan, USA.

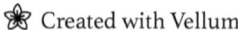 Created with Vellum

CONTENTS

Preface	v
1. The Pastor as Visionary Entrepreneur?	1
2. Visionary or Servant Leader?	7
3. Eldership	17
4. Shared Gift Ministry or Professional Elitism?	29
5. Accountability of Church Leaders	35
6. Women in Church Leadership	43
7. Paul's Prohibitions	51
8. The Importance of Keeping Watch	63
9. Oversight of Worship	71
10. Let's Scrap Church Vision Statements!	87
11. Changing the Narrative	93
Also by Kevin Simington	99
Someone Else's Life	101
The Starpath Series	103
Rethinking The Gospel	105
Making Sense of the Bible	107
No More Monkey Business:	109
Finding God When He Seems To Be Hiding	111
Welcome To The Universe	113
Leave A Review	115
Connect With Kevin Simington	117
About the Author	119
Notes	121

PREFACE

This is a little book. Hence the title. It is deliberately brief. My purpose is to provide a succinct treatment of this important subject so that the central message doesn't get drowned in a flood of verbiage. People who struggle to wade through a typically-sized book will find this little book an easy read. The chapters are short and the message has been distilled down to its crystalline essence.

And what is its central message?

There is a crisis of leadership within the modern church. I don't mean an absence of leadership. The modern church has plenty of leadership; just not always the right sort. The kind of leadership that has evolved in many churches today is a long way from the collaborative leadership that was taught in the New Testament and practised by the first century church. The modern church has absorbed a philosophy and style of leadership that is more attuned to the business world than to the Bible. This book is a call to seriously re-evaluate the church leadership style that has developed in recent decades and return to the patterns and principles of church leadership as outlined in the New Testament.

The chapters in this book were originally published as individual essays designed to stand alone. As a result, some scriptures and themes make an appearance in more than one chapter. I have retained this repetition, as it serves to reinforce the central theme of the book.

This is a little book with big ideas. Putting the New Testament principles of church leadership into practice would necessitate a revolution within many churches: that is how far many churches have strayed from the original biblical precepts. The big ideas in this little book could seriously shake up your church. But biblical truth is like that.

Are you ready to be challenged?

Read on.

1
THE PASTOR AS VISIONARY ENTREPRENEUR?

Visionary leadership is the "in thing" these days. Everyone is talking about it. Everyone wants it. Company boardrooms insist that their senior management team be visionary leaders. There is not a major company, business or charity that does not have a "vision statement". This trend has found its way into the church. Go into any Christian bookstore and you will find whole shelves of books devoted to visionary leadership in the church. When considering a prospective pastor, the question of whether he or she is a visionary leader is high on the agenda. It is now considered an essential quality if a church is to grow and be effective.

But I want to ask some important questions: Is visionary leadership Biblical? Does this model of leadership have its basis in God's Word or in the business world? As soon as I ask these kinds of questions, I am in danger of being labelled a narrow minded, anti-progressive fundamentalist. But it seems to me that the concept of visionary leadership has been swallowed unthinkingly by the Christian church with very little reflection upon its predicates, and with minimal corroboration with scripture.

WHAT IS MEANT BY VISIONARY LEADERSHIP?

The Centre for Visionary Leadership states, *"Visionary leaders are the builders of a new dawn, working with imagination, insight and boldness. They present a challenge that calls forth the best in people and brings them together around a shared sense of purpose. They work with the power of intentionality and alignment with a higher purpose. Their eyes are on the horizon, not just on the near at hand. They are social innovators and change agents, seeing the big picture and thinking strategically."* It also described entrepreneurial vision as *"imagining the future as one would wish it to be"*.

In other words, visionary leadership refers to the ability of an individual to envisage a different future, together with the ability to formulate and implement a plan to bring about the required changes. In essence, visionary leadership says, "This is how I would like things to be different in the future. This is what I would like the church to look like in 'x' years' time".

Undergirding this philosophy of visionary leadership is the concept that leadership via broad collaboration, consultation and consensus simply doesn't work. There is a strong belief within Christianity today that the most successful leadership is where one person, or a very small team of professional leaders, initiates, shapes and "casts" the vision, and then has the ability to inspire others to participate in that vision. Indeed, it is remarkable (and deeply concerning) how swiftly the modern church has acquiesced to this view of the elite, professional vision-casting leader.

THE SECULAR BASIS OF THE VISIONARY LEADERSHIP MODEL

In researching this chapter, I spent several hours reading over 30 articles on *"Visionary / Entrepreneurial Leadership In The Church"*, and what staggered me is the almost complete lack of scriptural justification for this leadership philosophy. Instead, there is a constant appeal to skills and strategies that have proved effective in the secular business world, and a rallying call for the church to get on board if we wish to be successful in growth and expansion. The current church emphasis on visionary leadership has drawn heavily, and unashamedly, from secular models.

Following the publication, in 1989, of Steven R. Covey's landmark secular book on leadership, *"Seven Habits of Highly Effective People"* (which has sold over 30 million copies), church leaders seized upon his principles, derived from the *business* world, and incorporated them into church life. A swathe of Christian leadership books soon followed, such as *"How Successful People Lead"*, by John C. Maxwell; *"The Conviction to Lead"*, by Albert Mohler; *"Courageous Leadership"*, by Bill Hybels; and the classic *"Spiritual Leadership"*, by J. Oswald Sanders. Literally hundreds of books on this topic were published within a few short years, and there would be very few pastors who would not have at least one such book on their shelves.

Evangelical author, Michael Horton, writes:

"Even those who accept the Bible's full trustworthiness on paper often do not see it as sufficient in matters of doctrine and Christian practice. Our real authorities are secular; judging by some of the most popular books being read by pastors these days."

Similarly, Orrel Steinkamp writes:

"Pastors are in a bind. The pervasive church-growth atmosphere tells them they must produce numerically, or they aren't cutting it; managerial marketers ply them with sure-fire techniques to produce those numbers. The Pastor-CEO should get with the program or go into another profession! It is assumed that a biblically based ministry, in itself, will just not get the job done".

Oz Guinness comments:

"The two most easily recognisable hallmarks of secularisation are the exaltation of numbers and technique. Both are prominent in the modern church-growth movement."

The tidal wave of literature promoting a "sanctified" version of secular leadership strategies within the church has had a profound impact on the perceived role of both clergy and laity. Of great concern is the increasingly common abrogation of congregational responsibility to prayerfully and collectively seek the guidance of God's Spirit in order to formulate wise and godly strategies for implementing the church's mission. Increasingly, this responsibility is now primarily seen as the domain of the "visionary" professional pastor and his close circle of staff members. It is this professional team who largely dream up the vision, set the direction and formulate the policies of many churches.

THE VISIONARY LEADER AND ENTREPRENEURIAL SKILLS

Integral to the concept of visionary leadership, is the necessity for vision to be accompanied by entrepreneurial skills. This refers to the ability of the leader to translate his vision into action through the use of highly effective skills imported from the business world. These skills include research, goal setting, marketing, branding, recruitment, vision casting, reinforcement and "selling" the church's product. Accordingly, the working week of today's entrepreneurial pastor is vastly different from that of pastors and ministers decades ago. Today's professional pastor spends far more time performing managerial and administrative tasks that are drawn directly from the secular realm of business CEO's and managers, and much less time in the pursuit of the traditional shepherding tasks that concerned their ministerial predecessors. The article, *"Why We Need More Entrepreneurial Church Leaders, Not More Shepherds"*, by Carey Nieuwhof, highlights the radical change that has occurred in the role of the professional pastor and exemplifies the current ecclesiological push for them to be skilled entrepreneurs. The requirement for professional pastors to exhibit expertise in a wide range of secular entrepreneurial skills has become almost mandatory for consideration of pastoral appointment in many churches.

The scriptural justification for this twofold philosophy, that the pastor is both visionary leader and savvy entrepreneur, is shaky at best. The most commonly cited Bible verse is Proverbs 29:18, *"Where there is no vision, the people perish"*. Proponents of this leadership philosophy also cite Abraham, Moses, Jesus and Paul as biblical examples of visionary leaders.

J. Oswald Sanders' book, *"Spiritual Leadership"*, was arguably the most influential book in convincing and converting Christian leaders in the 20th century to this philosophy. One paragraph of his book was recently quoted to a friend of mine by his pastor in an attempt to prove the biblical basis of visionary leadership:

"Those who have most powerfully and permanently influenced their generation have been "seers" – men who have seen more and further than others. Men of faith, for faith is vision. This was true of the prophets or seers of the Old Testament times. Moses, one of the greatest leaders of all time, "Endured as seeing Him who is invisible." His faith imparted vision. Elisha's servant saw with great vividness the vastness of the encircling army. Elisha saw the invincible environing host of heaven who were invisible to his servant. His faith imparted vision."

But how valid is this view of leadership? Is this truly the New Testament model of leadership? That is the topic of the next chapter.

2

VISIONARY OR SERVANT LEADER?

God has always led his church by raising up human leaders. The church is not a democracy: it is a theocracy, with God as the ultimate authority, guiding and governing his people through wise and godly human leaders. This was certainly the case throughout the Old Testament and continued to be the case within the burgeoning New Testament church, initially through the wise oversight of the Apostles and, subsequently, through the eventual establishment of groups of elders within individual churches. The biblical antecedent and practical necessity of wise, godly leadership within the church is not in question. What *is* in question, however, is the *style* of leadership.

In the previous chapter, I outlined the radical change in the perceived role of the professional pastor in recent decades, from shepherd to entrepreneurial, visionary leader. This change was precipitated by the influx of leadership books in the 1980's which adapted secular managerial and leadership strategies from the business world and incorporated them into church life. Clergy are now expected to be the main "vision casters" and to excel in a wide range of entrepreneurial skills, the effectiveness of which is thought to significantly impact the growth and success of the church as a whole.

Visionary leadership refers to the ability of an individual to envisage a different future, together with the ability to formulate and implement a plan to bring about the required change. In essence, visionary leadership says, *"This is how I would like things to be different in the future. This is what I would like the church to look like in 'x' years' time"*.

But how valid is this view of leadership? Is this truly the biblical model of leadership?

ASSESSING THE SCRIPTURAL VALIDITY OF VISIONARY LEADERSHIP

The scriptural justification for this philosophy of visionary, entrepreneurial leadership is shaky at best. The most commonly cited Bible verse is Proverbs 29:18, *"Where there is no vision, the people perish"*. Proponents of this leadership philosophy also cite Abraham, Moses, Elijah, Jesus and Paul as biblical examples of visionary leaders. So, let us examine the scriptural justification of this pervasive philosophy.

PROVERBS 29:18

The King James version of this particular verse is the most

commonly cited, because it uses the word "vision": *"Where there is no vision, the people perish"*. There are two problems with the way this verse is often quoted. **Firstly**, according to the most recent textual scholarship, the word "vision" is not considered to be the best translation of the Hebrew (chazon: חָזוֹן). The NIV and TNIV provide us with a more accurate rendering:

"Where there is no revelation, people cast off restraint"

Secondly, the second half of the verse is usually ignored. The complete verse is

"Where there is no revelation, people cast off restraint,

but blessed are those who heed wisdom's instruction."

This proverb is written using classic Hebrew parallelism. In parallelism, the two halves of a proverb describe the same truth, either by similarity or by contrast. In this case, the conjunction "but" indicates that contrast is intended. When God's *"revelation"* is absent or not heeded, people's behaviour degenerates, but when *"wisdom's instruction"* is heeded, people are blessed. In this parallelism, therefore, we are meant to understand that *"revelation"* and *"wisdom's instruction"* are one and the same thing. The first line of the parallelism describes the consequences of ignoring God's instructions, while the second line describe the benefits of heeding them. What is being described here is not some esoteric vision of the future, not some conjured up imagining by an individual of what they would like to see happen one day, but the publicly revealed words of God, declared to

His people to guide their behaviour. This verse is proclaiming the importance of sound biblical teaching that provides moral and theological guidance for God's people.

To quote this verse as a justification for the contemporary philosophy of "visionary leadership" is lifting the verse out of context and completely ignoring many of the basic principles of hermeneutics (principles of biblical interpretation). In fact, this verse teaches the EXACT OPPOSITE of visionary leadership! It exhorts us to be people who read and obey God's Word rather than following our own agendas.

SUPPOSED VISIONARY LEADERS IN THE BIBLE

Let us turn our attention to the Bible characters who are often cited as examples of people who embodied visionary leadership. As we do so, let me reiterate our working definition: visionary leadership refers to the ability of an individual to envisage a different future, together with the ability to formulate and implement a plan to bring about the required change. Now, we must ask the important question: do any of the commonly cited Bible characters demonstrate this ability?

MOSES

God appeared to Moses in a physical manifestation known, in theological terms, as a theophany. In this case it was a burning bush, but there have been many different theophanies: a pillar of cloud, a pillar of fire, a thunder cloud, a gentle wind, a shining light, and several human manifestations (the visitors to Abraham, Jacob's wrestler and, finally, Jesus Christ). When God appeared to Moses, he outlined his plan to rescue the Israelites. He commanded Moses to go to Pharaoh and ask for Israel's release. But Moses tried to wriggle out of it. He gave several excuses as to why he wasn't suited and why it wasn't a good plan but, in the end, he reluctantly agreed. When the rescue mission was well underway, and things began to turn sour, Moses took his complaint to God, reminding Him that the people and the plan were <u>His</u> (God's) idea and that he (Moses) was being left to 'carry the can':

"Moses said to the LORD, "You have been telling me, 'Lead these people,' but you have not let me know whom you will send with me. You have said, 'I know you by name and you have found favour with me.' If you are pleased with me, teach me your ways so I may know you and continue to find favour with you. Remember that this nation is your people."" (Exodus 33:12-13)

This is not the language of a visionary leader who is implementing his own grand plan, but of a servant on an errand who has found himself in difficulties. Indeed, it was always God's plan, never Moses'. This is indicated by the frequent occurrence in the Exodus narrative of the phrase *"The LORD said to Moses"*. This phrase occurs 137 times in the book of Exodus, and each time it is followed by a command such as *"go"*, *"tell"*, *"return"*, *"say"*, *"take"*, *"build"*, *"strike"*, *"get"* etc. – commands of the kind a master would give his servant. Indeed, God refers to Moses as *"my servant"* on several occasions.

Moses was not a visionary leader. He was an obedient servant. The writer to the Hebrews acknowledges this when he writes, *"Moses was faithful as a <u>servant</u> in all God's house"* (Hebrews 3:5).

A good friend, Ken Collins, recently wrote:

"Moses was no utopian dreamer fired with revolutionary zeal to 'Free the People.' He wasn't the leader of the Popular Front for the Liberation of Goshen like some ancient Yasser Arafat. Much less was he the C.E.O. of 'Israel Incorporated' with a vision and strategy to move their operation 'off-shore' to Canaan. He was God's faithful servant."

It is servant leadership that Moses embodies, not visionary, entrepreneurial leadership. While this distinction might appear subtle to some, it is anything but! (More about this later).

ABRAHAM

Abraham did not formulate a grand plan to lead his people out of Haran. When he left his home-town, he did not even know where he was going:

"By faith Abraham, when called to go to a place he would later receive as his inheritance, obeyed and went, even though he did not know where he was going." (Hebrews 11: 8)

Abraham did not concoct this plan. He did not dream up a vision of a better life in a new land, and then convince everyone else that it was a great idea. There is absolutely no evidence of visionary leadership here, no evidence of *initiative*, just simple obedience to the call of God.

JESUS

Jesus came to earth to implement God's great rescue plan for mankind. Throughout his ministry, Jesus continually asserted that he was doing his Father's will, not his own. He did not come of his own accord, did not do his own work, did not choose his own disciples, nor even speak his own words:

"I have come down from heaven, not to do my own will, but to do the will of Him who sent me" (John 6:38)

"My food is to do the will of Him who sent me" (John 4:34)

"I do exactly what the Father has commanded me" (John 14:31)

"Truly, truly, I tell you, the Son can do nothing by himself, unless he sees the Father doing it. For whatever the Father does, the Son also does." (John 5:19)

"I do not seek my own will, but the will of Him who sent me" (John 5:30)

"The words I speak to you are not my own. Instead, it is the Father dwelling in me who is performing his works." (John 14:10)

At every point Jesus wants us to understand that He is not implementing his own plans or speaking his own words: he is simply obeying the will of His Heavenly Father. His entire three years of ministry was one of complete submission and obedience to the Father's will.

Ken Collins writes:

"Like Moses, our Lord was sent into the world to lead a rescue mission. It was not some vague vision with an equally vague strategy that afforded the ideal opportunity for Him to display His leadership skills, but a perfect plan that had been worked out in full and final detail before the foundation of the world and which would succeed only if followed to the letter. If He had chosen to deviate from the path; to ad-lib instead of following the script; to exercise His own initiative instead of simply following instructions, the whole plan would have failed. Because Jesus chose to obey, we can learn nothing about vision and strategy by looking at Him as we could learn nothing from Moses before Him. Vision and strategy are the companions of innovation and self-assertion not of obedience and submission. It is not possible to simultaneously model both obedience and initiative in the things of God."

Jesus was not a visionary leader, in the modern sense of the term. He was an obedient servant.

THE APOSTLE PAUL

At last we come to a Bible character who was a visionary leader! Saul (as he was initially called) *did* have a grand plan; one which he had formulated on his ***own initiative***. He was going to rid the world of Christians! His plan was well underway when God stepped in and put a stop to it. Paul was punished and humbled. He was then made to submit to God's plan, which he spent the rest of his life obediently implementing. As an Apostle, Paul was not a visionary, entrepreneurial leader; he too was an obedient servant.

SERVANT LEADERSHIP

Throughout the Bible, what we see is servant leadership, rather than visionary leadership. John MacArthur's classic, "*The Book on Leadership*", provides an excellent treatise on the biblical model of leadership. The difference between these two styles of leadership is not one of mere semantics; they are diametrically opposed. The kind of biblical leadership embodied in Moses, Paul and Jesus, is a far cry from the visionary, entrepreneurial leadership that keeps modern pastors ensconced in their offices, consumed with managerial tasks. Modern day visionary leadership involves implementing *my* will, *my* plans, *my* dreams, via cleverly constructed strategies that I have devised, and then convincing others to join with me. Servant leadership, on the other hand, involves laying aside my own schemes and obeying God's will, putting his plans and purposes into effect.

"But my plan is God's plan!" says the modern, visionary leader. *"He has revealed it to me, and now I am sharing it with you!"* I have two brief points to make regarding this kind of claim:

Firstly, I have been a member of churches long enough to see pastors come and go, each of whom has a different "*vision from God*" for the church. How is it, then, that when a new pastor comes to a church, his vision - his anointed plan - is always different from his predecessor's? Over the decades I have seen individual churches pulled one way, then another, pushed from pillar to post by successive pastors who come and go, each with a different vision, apparently from God. Does God keep changing his mind? No. This simply illustrates the fact that each pastor's vision for the church is his *own*, not God's. There is no other explanation! Although each pastor may well have a sincere desire to serve God and extend His kingdom, he is also deeply influenced by his own inclinations, preferences, biases, personal tastes and individual proclivities. It is *unavoidable* that any plan or vision for the church which is formulated by a single individual, no matter how prayerfully, is bound to have a lot of "him" or "her" in it.

Secondly, I am convinced that the New Testament model of church leadership is a collaborative one, rather than the "lone ranger" style that is proposed by modern, visionary leadership philosophy. In contrast to the Old Testament, where God's Spirit only rested upon individual anointed leaders, all God's people are now indwelt by the Holy Spirit and have direct access to God. Leadership, while still important in the New Testament church, is no longer the domain of individual, anointed prophets. Accordingly, the New Testament portrays a gradual evolution in its ecclesiology, culminating in the pastoral epistles which prescribe the appointment of a collaborative team of leaders in each church, comprised of elders and pastors (Acts 13:1-3; 14:23; Titus 1:5). ***This*** is the New Testament model for church leadership. This collaborative model provides protection against any single person's well-meaning but skewed preferences dominating a church. It also provides ultimate protection against a single "visionary leader" leading a church into error and heresy.

The vital role of elders as leaders of God's church is the topic of the next chapter.

3
ELDERSHIP

The New Testament model of church leadership is a collaborative one, rather than the *"lone ranger"* style proposed by the modern visionary leadership philosophy. It provides ultimate protection against a single "visionary leader" leading a church into error and heresy. It also protects a church from being "ping-ponged" from one visionary plan to another by the succession of pastors who come and go over the years.

Several terms are used by the New Testament to refer to church leaders, the most common being *"elders"* (*presbyteros*) and *"overseers"* (*episkopos*). These two terms describe the same office, as is evident by the way in which the two terms are sometimes used interchangeably (*Titus 1:5, 7; Acts 20:17, 28; 1 Timothy 3:1-2*). A third term is also sometimes used; the Greek word *"poimen"* (ποιμήν). This word literally means "*shepherd*" in Greek, the Latin translation of which is "*pastor*". The fact that the Latin translation of the word has found its way into many modern English translations is unfortunate because of the connotations of professional office that the term "*pastor*" has absorbed over the centuries. The New Testament Christians, however, reading this Greek word "*shepherd*" (centuries before the Latin term "*pastor*" was applied) would have understood its implications implicitly.

This term, "poimen" (shepherd), is imagery drawn directly from the fields of Israel. Are you aware of the two primary roles of a shepherd? The shepherd of a flock of sheep:

- Protects the flock from marauding predators

- Ensures that the flock are fed adequately, by leading them to good pasture

It is important to note that the primary role of the shepherd is not to spend his time going from sheep to sheep, cuddling individual sheep! Have you ever seen a shepherd do that? No. The shepherd's primary job is to lead, feed and protect. The same is true in God's church. The shepherd or elder is not primarily a pastoral visitor or a counsellor, although when an individual "sheep" is in crisis the elder may be called upon to visit and pray with that sheep. But primarily, he or she is called by God to protect the church from false doctrine and to ensure that they are fed the truth of God's word. This is their primary responsibility, to which God will ultimately hold them accountable:

"... they watch over you as those who must give an account" (Hebrews 13:17)

The shepherd is one who watches over and cares for God's flock, with the understanding that Christ is the head shepherd.

The Apostle Peter uses all three terms – shepherd, elder and overseer - to refer to the leaders of God's church when he says:

*"To the **elders** (presbyteros) among you, I appeal as a fellow **elder** and a witness of Christ's sufferings who also will share in the glory to be revealed: Be **shepherds** (poimen) of God's flock that is under your care, **overseeing** (episkopos) them—not because you must, but because you are willing, as God wants you to be; not pursuing dishonest gain, but eager to serve; <u>not lording it over</u> those entrusted to you, but being examples to the flock. And when the Chief **Shepherd** appears, you will receive the crown of glory that will never fade away." (1 Peter 5:1-4)*

A swathe of excellent books has been published describing the biblical role of elders, and I don't intend to plunge into a detailed exposition of that information here. In summary, however, elders are to teach (*1 Timothy 3:2; 5:17; 1 Peter 5:2*); to guard (*Acts 20:28-29; Titus 1:9-14*); to oversee (*1 Peter 5:3; Hebrews 13:7, 17*); to handle disputes (*Acts 15:2ff*); to visit and pray for the sick (*James 5:14*) and to supervise the distribution of money (*Acts 11:30*). I feel no need to replicate the already existing detailed analysis of these roles, except to make three important points:

1. **The leadership of elders / overseers / shepherds is not to be domineering.** Peter, in the passage, quoted above, portrays a very balanced view of eldership authority. On the one hand, they are not to *"lord it over"* their flock in an authoritarian, domineering way (*verse 3*). On the other hand, in the verse that immediately follows on from this passage, Peter urges the church at large to *"submit yourselves to your elders"* (*1 Peter 5:5*). Both of these truths need to be held in tension; churches must allow their elderships to lead, and elders must do so with servant-hearted love and humility.

2. **The primary function of the shepherd / elder is not to cuddle the sheep, but to keep them *safe*.** The elder is to ensure that the flock are not led astray by false teaching:

"<u>Keep watch</u> over yourselves and over all the flock, among which the Holy Spirit has made you overseers, to shepherd the church of God which He purchased with His own blood. I know that after my departure savage wolves will come in among you, not sparing the flock; and from among your own selves men will arise, <u>speaking perverse things</u>, to draw away the disciples after them. (Acts 20:28-30).

Thus, when outlining the essential characteristics of a potential elder, Paul writes that:

"He <u>must hold firmly to the trustworthy message</u> as it has been taught, so that he can encourage others by <u>sound doctrine</u> and <u>refute those who oppose it</u>" (Titus 1:9).

Elsewhere, Paul writes that it is essential that the elder be *"able to teach"* (1 Tim 3:2).

To summarise, the primary role of elders is to ensure the teaching of sound doctrine, to defend the truth and to refute error. This is what is meant by the injunction to *"keep watch over all the flock" (Acts 20:28)*. The writer to the Hebrews describes the seriousness of this eldership task when he writes:

"They keep watch over you as those who must give an account [to God]" (Heb 13:17).

Thus, according to the New Testament, everything that is preached and taught within the church must come under the oversight and scrutiny of the entire eldership, for they will ultimately be held to account for it by God. This does not mean that every elder should be a gifted preacher, but it does mean that the *entire* eldership must be collaboratively involved in formulating and reviewing the church's preaching and teaching program, including providing ongoing evaluation and feedback for those who do the preaching and teaching. This oversight is not limited to the Sunday sermon, but extends to everything that is taught within the full scope of the church's various programs. The common tendency of many elderships to "sub-contract" this teaching oversight to paid pastors is an abrogation of their God-given responsibility and a direct contradiction of the teaching of the New Testament.

3. The qualifications for being appointed as an elder require more than simply a godly character. Inherent in the scriptural injunctions for elders to oversee the teaching within a church, is the necessity for elders to be mature in the faith, knowledgeable in God's Word, with a thorough grasp of sound doctrine. It is not enough for a prospective elder to have a godly character; that is merely the starting point. A prospective elder must also excel in the areas of biblical knowledge, doctrinal comprehension and spiritual wisdom. The elder must be able to articulate sound doctrine, competently evaluate biblical teaching, identify error and refute false or misleading teaching. This is what Paul means when he says that an elder must be *"able to teach"* (*1 Timothy 3:2*). Paul identifies this essential quality of elders even more clearly in Titus 1:9, when he says, *"the elder is to encourage others with sound doctrine and refute those who oppose it."* All of this infers not only significant doctrinal knowledge, but also a strength of character that enables the elder to confidently engage in complex dialogue and theological debate if necessary. Sadly, over the years, I have seen many people appointed to eldership who, while exhibiting a godly character, are biblically and doctrinally naive, and who are not qualified at all to guard God's flock.

ELDERSHIP AS A PLURALITY

Here we come to the crux of the matter. The New Testament never envisages a situation where a church is led by a solo elder / shepherd, *even if that shepherd is paid a salary*. There is simply no hint in scripture of an individual single-handedly formulating and implementing a church's preaching program, determining church policy and deciding the "vision" for the church. The Bible does not advocate "sub-contracting" these responsibilities to a single paid pastor. In every instance in the New Testament when a church's leadership structure is described, it is very clearly a collaborative plurality of elders / shepherds / overseers. This is true even in the initial years of the church when it was led by the Apostles themselves:

• In **Acts 6** the church was faced with the problem of widows who were being overlooked in the daily administration of food. The apostles came to a ***collective*** decision to appoint deacons to oversee this ministry, and their decision found approval by the whole congregation. Importantly, as well as illustrating the collective nature of decision-making, this incident also reveals that providing practical pastoral care to church members was <u>not</u> regarded by the Apostles as the responsibility of those who are in eldership.

• **Acts 13** describes the leadership team at Antioch as being comprised of *"prophets and teachers"*, five of whom are specifically named (Acts 13:1). The next verse describes how the whole team sensed God's leading to set apart Barnabas and Saul for missionary work. Once again, it is collaborative decision-making that is in evidence.

• **Acts 14** records that as Paul and Barnabas travelled on their missionary journey, they *"appointed elders in every church"* (*Acts 14:23*). Plurality of leadership was essential in ensuring balanced oversight of each church.

• **Acts 15** describes a crucial decision facing the early church. What expectations should be placed upon Gentile converts regarding adherence to Judaic Law? The decision was made by the *"apostles and elders"* in the church in Jerusalem (*Acts 15:4, 6, 22, 23*). Even in this early stage in the church's development, elders had been added to the leadership team in Jerusalem, to share the leadership of the church, alongside the Apostles. In Luke's narrative of this event, he particularly points out that the Apostles and elders were *"of one mind"* regarding their decision (Acts 15:25), indicating that the decision was arrived at via consensus and unity. This passage is very important for our understanding of the role of professional pastors today. **Even the great Apostle Peter did not have authority to unilaterally make decisions and set policy.**

• **Acts 20** describes Paul meeting with the elders of the church at Ephesus as Paul was on his way to Rome. Although Timothy, the itinerant preacher and evangelist and Paul's co-worker, seems to have had a key preaching role at Ephesus (1 Timothy 1:3), there remained a wider leadership team of elders who led the church (Acts 20:17-38).

• In **Titus 1:5**, Paul reminds Titus of the crucial task that he commissioned Titus with: *"The reason I left you in Crete was that you would set in order what was unfinished and appoint **elders** in every town, as I directed you."* The absolute necessity for plurality of leadership in each church was non-negotiable in Paul's mind (see also *Philippians 1:1; Jas 5:14*).

THE IMPORTANCE OF A PLURALITY OF ELDERS

A plurality of elders within a church is essential for the safety and well-being of God's flock. Why?

1. No one man (or woman) has all the wisdom and gifts necessary to lead God's church. The paid pastor needs a team of fellow shepherds to add their gifts and insights to his limited abilities. This will ensure that the church's ministry is not "lop-sided" and skewed towards one individual's preferences and gift areas.

2. The elders need to hold each other accountable for their lifestyle and their teaching. The paid pastor is not exempt from this; he is just as accountable to his fellow elders as they are to him. This level of mutual accountability is essential if the church is to be protected from drifting into theological error or moral sin. Inherent in this relationship of accountability is the necessity for elders to be willing to correct and even rebuke the paid pastor if necessary, and also for the paid pastor to be willing to submit himself to that level of accountability. The Apostle Paul demonstrated his willingness to correct the teaching of a fellow elder when he confronted the Apostle Peter about his wrong teaching: *"But when Peter came to Antioch, I opposed him to his face, because he was in error"* (Galatians 2:11).

3. A plurality of elders is much more likely to collaboratively discern the will of God. It disconcertingly easy for one person to mistakenly interpret his own inclinations as the leading of God's Spirit. But when a team of elders prayerfully arrive at a consensus regarding God's leading in a matter, the church can have considerably more assurance that God's will has been correctly discerned. Conversely, a church that is led by a single, dominating figure is much more likely to be led astray, either theologically or in its practice.

THE DANGER OF SOLO LEADERSHIP

Significantly, there is only one church mentioned in the New Testament that appears to have been dominated by a single, dictatorial leader and the result was disastrous. There is a reference to this church and its leader in John's third Epistle, which he wrote to address some deeply concerning developments there. The church in question was located somewhere in Asia and was dominated by a man called Diotrephes. John had previously sent itinerant preachers throughout Asia, visiting each of the churches in that area to strengthen and encourage them. But in one church, its egotistical solo leader, Diotrephes, had rejected the itinerant preachers and had even excommunicated any church members who showed them hospitality. Consequently, the Apostle John wrote:

"I wrote to the church, but Diotrephes, who loves to be first, will not welcome us. So when I come, I will call attention to what he is doing, spreading malicious lies about us. Not satisfied with that, he even refuses to welcome other believers. He also stops those who want to do so and puts them out of the church. Dear friends, do not imitate what is evil." (3 John 1:9-11)

It is a rather scathing denunciation of a dictatorial solo leader who has somehow seized control of a church and is acting selfishly and arrogantly, implementing his own egotistical agenda without accountability or collaboration. John's statement that Diotrephes "loves to be first" is a disturbingly accurate assessment of the kind of person who can sometimes assume domineering control of a church if a strong, collaborative leadership team is not in place.

THE NEED TO RESTORE BIBLICAL ELDERSHIP

The modern church has drifted away from the model of Biblical eldership:

- Some churches do not have elders at all and have granted their professional clergy almost absolute power in determining church policy and practice. In these churches, so long as the pastor doesn't move the organ, sell the church building or rearrange the sanctuary, he can almost do as he likes. He is certainly not held to account regarding the accuracy of his teaching or the godliness of his lifestyle, nor does anyone feel they have the right to challenge his philosophy of ministry. After all, he is the professional!

- Other churches have elderships in name only. In many churches, elders are regarded as being little more than glorified deacons, having little authority, no sense of mutual accountability with the paid pastor and very little understanding of their God-ordained mutual responsibility to lead the church. They are often elected because of their caring hearts and their loyalty to the pastor. Pastors often nominate elders who are already "on their side" and who will support them unquestioningly. Consequently, many elderships see their primary role as supporting and protecting the pastor, rather than as leading and guarding God's church. They certainly don't understand their responsibility to critique, question, or even challenge the pastor regarding his teaching or policies.

In his classic book, "*Biblical Eldership: An Urgent Call To Restore Biblical Church Leadership*" Alexander Strauch presents a heartfelt plea for the modern church to abandon its unquestioning trust in the "Pastor-as-CEO" model and return to the biblical roots of leadership via eldership. I whole-heartedly agree!

4
SHARED GIFT MINISTRY OR PROFESSIONAL ELITISM?

I received two completely opposite emails while I was writing this chapter. The first was very encouraging. It was from a friend who is a pastor of a church in another state. He described to me how, over a period of time, he has identified those within his congregation whom God has gifted to preach, and he has enfolded them into the preaching ministry of his church. He wrote:

"I've put together a preaching team who meet regularly to plan our preaching program and also to assess and give feedback on each other's preaching."

I was thrilled to hear of a "professional" pastor who not only recognises that God gives preaching gifts to lay people but is secure enough to allow them to play a significant role in the church's preaching ministry!

The second email was not so encouraging. In fact, it was the complete opposite. It was from a friend who is a retired pastor, who was, and still is, a very gifted preacher. He still feels called to preach, but the young pastor of the church where he now attends (who is not a particularly competent preacher) only asks him to preach once or twice a year. I had previously written to this friend regarding the biblical model of pastors encouraging and utilising the gifts that God places within the church. He replied:

"Unfortunately, I don't see that model working at [name of church]. There is a strong professional elitism here where the pastor's preaching is beyond congregational accountability, where feedback is not welcome, and lay people such as me, are largely locked out of any significant input into preaching ministry, irrespective of one's giftedness. It is a constant source of frustration for me, as I feel called to continue to preach and to have an input into that ministry. If God brings gifted Bible teachers to a church, why don't full-time pastors want to work with them??? Pastors say they believe in the gift ministry of the body, but in practise they deny this by monopolising certain key gift areas. My frustration is exacerbated by the fact that [pastor's name] is not a particularly gifted preacher, so I often sit there extremely frustrated as he skims across the surface of a passage while doing violence to the accepted principles of biblical interpretation."

Sadly, this scenario is not uncommon in the modern church. I recently (and unexpectedly) met up with a past ministry colleague who is now retired. He was, and still is, one of the most gifted preachers I know. As we chatted, I asked him whether he was preaching regularly in his local church (pastored by a relatively young man). He lamented that he was only asked to preach in that church a couple of times each year (when the pastor was on holidays), because the pastor liked to do all the preaching himself. I came away from that meeting deeply saddened that such a gifted preacher, still at the "top of his game", was effectively locked out of significant ministry in his own church.

These two sad stories reflect a commonly held belief among many clergy today that "the professional" must do all or most of the preaching, even if there are others within the congregation who are equally or more gifted in that area. This is a perplexing contradiction, because if you asked these pastors *"Do you believe in the gift ministry of the body?"* they would almost certainly agree. They have probably even preached many sermons on the "gift passages" of the Bible (*1 Corinthians 12, Romans 12 and Ephesians 4*). Yet, in practice, they exclude the laity from key gift areas that they perceive as being the domain of the professionals.

This, of course, is contrary to the role of the pastor, as outlined in Ephesians 4. This passage clearly specifies that the role of the pastor is **not** to do all the ministry himself, but to *"equip God's people for works of service" (Ephesians 4:12)*. In other words, the pastor's **primary** role is to identify and encourage the giftings of church members. Hence, Paul instructs the leaders of the church in Rome, *"if it is teaching, let him teach" (Romans 12:7)*. Encouraging and developing the gift ministry of the laity should not be limited to welcoming, ushering, prayer chains and pastoral visitation. A pastor who is faithfully fulfilling his calling to foster the gift ministry of the whole body of Christ should also be developing a growing team of preachers within his congregation.

THE BIBLICAL MODEL OF SHARED GIFT MINISTRY

We see this model clearly portrayed in the growing team of preachers in the church at Antioch, recorded for us in the book of Acts:

• **Acts 11:20-21.** Some un-named Christians from Cyprus and Cyrene settled in Antioch and began to preach the gospel, resulting in a steady harvest.

• **Acts 11:22-24.** The church in Jerusalem heard about what was happening in Antioch and sent Barnabas to help with the preaching. Under the combined preaching of this enlarged team *"a great number of people were brought to the Lord" (v.24)*

• **Acts 11:25-26.** The church grew so rapidly that Barnabas felt the need for further gifted preachers, so he travelled to Tarsus and brought the newly converted Saul back to Antioch. With Saul's addition to the preaching team, they *"taught great numbers of people" (v.26)*.

• **Acts 11:27-30.** Some *"prophets"* moved from Jerusalem to Antioch and added their public proclamations to the teaching ministry. One of them, named Agabus, was used by God to predict a famine in Judea *(v.28)*, to which the church in Antioch responded by sending a love offering to the elders of the churches in Judea *(vv.29-30)*.

- **Acts 12:25-13:3.** John Mark came from Jerusalem to Antioch, at the instigation of Barnabas and Saul, to join the preaching team. At this point, Luke lists the key members of the preaching team in Antioch: *"Now in the church at Antioch there were prophets and teachers: Barnabas, Simeon called Niger, Lucius of Cyrene, Manaen (who had been brought up with Herod the tetrarch) and Saul"* as well as *"John Mark" (12:25 - 13:1)*.

The growth in the preaching team in Antioch over this period of time was considerable: some un-named Christians + Barnabas + Saul + some prophets (including Agabus) + John Mark + Simeon + Manaen + Lucius. While some of these were "imported" from Jerusalem, others were clearly raised up from within the church. It is also important to note that these people weren't professional clergy. Each of them would have had to work to support themselves (as Paul later testified – 1 Corinthians 4:12; 1 Thessalonians 2:9; Acts 20:34).

The church in Antioch is a wonderful model of shared gift ministry, as a growing number of gifted teachers and prophets were added to the preaching team. Barnabas and Saul did not seek to monopolise or dominate this ministry but welcomed each one as God raised them up.

THE CHALLENGE TO THE MODERN CHURCH

The early church in Antioch should be a model for us to follow. If God places people with certain gifts within a congregation, he intends those gifts to be utilised. The responsibility of paid pastors is to identify, encourage and facilitate gift ministry within their congregation, rather than to stifle it. My friend's assertion that *"Pastors say they believe in the gift ministry of the body, but in practice they deny this by monopolising certain key gift areas"* is all too often true. The modern, professional clergy have developed an elitist mindset in regard to preaching. This may not be entirely their fault, as congregations can have the attitude, *"That's what we pay the professionals to do"*.

But the gift of teaching and preaching is not distributed by God on the basis of church salary. The Holy Spirit distributes these gifts *"according to his will"* (1 Cor 12:11). Pastors who, as a result of their own egos and insecurities, defensively monopolise the preaching ministry in their church, are robbing their church of the rich diversity of gifts and teaching that the Holy Spirit wishes to bring. They are also robbing themselves of the blessing of working with, and learning from, other gifted preachers.

As my friend asked in his email, *"If God brings gifted Bible teachers to a church, why don't full-time pastors want to work with them???"* That is an excellent question. Why indeed?

Finishing on a positive note, when my pastor friend from inter-state wrote to me about the preaching team he had developed in his church, I replied:

"That is SO encouraging to hear that you have developed a preaching team and that you regularly meet for planning, accountability and feedback! Wow! Well done you! I believe that is a thoroughly biblical model."

May many more churches follow in his footsteps.

5

ACCOUNTABILITY OF CHURCH LEADERS

No one in Christian leadership should be above accountability. In fact, the more prominent one's leadership role, the more important accountability becomes – for the sake of the leader and that of the whole church. It is essential that Christian leaders develop close accountability relationships in which they are regularly held to account in the areas of time usage, ministry activities, preaching, theology, personal spirituality, ethics and morality.

Many parachurch organisations now have weekly, structured accountability meetings for their staff, where very specific questions are asked. For example, within Chuck Swindoll's organisation, *Insight For Living*, each staff member has a weekly meeting with a colleague where they are asked the following questions:

1. Have you been with a woman anywhere this past week that might be seen as compromising?

2. Have any of your financial dealings lacked integrity?

3. Have you exposed yourself to any sexually explicit material?

4. Have you spent adequate time in Bible study and prayer?

5. Have you given priority time to your family?

6. Have you fulfilled the mandates of your calling?

7. Have you just lied to me?

Many parachurch organisations have now mandated this kind of regular interview for staff. These kinds of accountability questions, however, are not a recent phenomenon. In the 1700's, John Wesley's colleagues were expected to answer the following questions each week:

1. What known sins have you committed since our last meeting?

2. What temptations have you met with?

3. How were you delivered?

4. What have you thought, said, or done, of which you doubt whether it be sin or not?

5. Have you nothing you desire to keep secret?

While modern parachurch organisations are leading the way in this sort of structured accountability, pastoral ministry in the local church is lagging a long way behind. Many local church pastors, particularly senior pastors, have little or no accountability at any deep, personal level. Sadly, this sometimes has tragic results.

The recent revelation that the senior pastor of a megachurch in America had a 10-year affair with a woman in his church is one such tragedy. After the woman came forward and reported the affair, two other female ex-staff workers also reported that the pastor had tried to seduce them. Several associate pastors have now left the church over this issue. This is just one of a long list of ministry tragedies that might have been avoided had there been rigorous weekly accountability relationships in place.

Some denominations have sought to address this issue by encouraging their pastors to form buddy relationships with another pastor within the denomination, for the purpose of meeting together occasionally for accountability and support. Other denominations have appointed a "pastor to pastors" whose job it is to visit pastors for the same purpose. Both of these models, however, have failed dismally, for three reasons.

1. In some cases these meetings never take place or cease to take place after a short period of time.

2. If the meetings do take place, they are usually spasmodic or too infrequent, and tend to diminish over time.

3. Even in the case of regular meetings, the accountability relationship is completely removed from the local church scene. The "accountability buddy" is not part of the same church and cannot give any accurate, detailed feedback on

the minister's ministry and conduct. The buddy is totally dependent on the honesty and insight of the pastor's self-reflection.

Any meaningful accountability relationship for church leaders *must* be based within the local church itself. Unfortunately, in the case of the professional pastor, there are several obstacles blocking this kind of relationship from forming:

1. A perceived lack of a suitable "accountability buddy" candidate within the congregation. A pastor may feel that there is no-one suitably mature whom he respects and trusts to form this relationship.

2. An unwillingness or awkwardness on the part of members of the congregation to ask their pastor the tough questions.

3. An elitist view of the professional ministry. This is a deeply ingrained attitude within both pastors and congregations in the modern church. Some pastors view themselves as being "above" congregational scrutiny, because of their specialist training, anointed calling and professional status. Congregations often perpetuate this divide by attaching to pastors an Old Testament-styled priestly status. Having experienced both sides of this divide myself (having been both a lay member and a professional pastor) I am convinced that even in the most humble of pastors, there often resides a subtle, yet insidious attitude whereby the pastor sees himself as quite separate from the congregation, as if he exists on another plane that is beyond the understanding of the average lay person.

In many ways, the modern clergy / laity distinction has perpetuated a divide which undermines the truth that we are all simply brothers and sisters in God's family. We are **all** now priests in the Kingdom of God (1 Peter 2:5-9), with **equal** access to God's Spirit (Acts 2:17-18). We **all** have equal access to God's truth and wisdom. For this reason, the Bible exhorts us:

"Let the Word of Christ dwell among you richly, as you <u>teach and admonish one another with all wisdom</u>" (Colossians 3:16).

This biblical concept of mutual accountability is a **vital** concept that the church must embrace. The clergy do **not** have a monopoly on wisdom and maturity. Spiritual maturity and wisdom have **nothing** to do with whether one's salary is paid by the church or by a secular company. Over the years I have encountered many wise, mature Christians who work in the secular workforce, and many professional clergy who are distinctly lacking in wisdom and maturity.

The priest / laity distinction was an Old Testament concept that was rendered obsolete on the day of Pentecost, when the Holy Spirit indwelt <u>*every*</u> Christian. Sadly, the concept of the Old Testament priestly office has crept back into the modern church. While it is right and proper for some people to be set apart for full time paid service, we must be constantly vigilant against any hint of spiritual elitism. The fact that some of God's servants are paid a salary by the church does not automatically make them wiser or more mature than a brother or sister who earns a salary elsewhere. Indeed, many young pastors have a lot to learn from older, more mature brothers and sisters in Christ.

Mutual accountability acknowledges the fact that God's wisdom does not reside in just a few individuals within a church; it dwells among us communally:

"Let the Word of Christ dwell among you richly, as you teach and admonish one another with all wisdom" (Col 3:16).

As brothers and sisters, with equal access to the Spirit of God, we are equally responsible to hold each other to account, for the sake of our own well-being and that of the whole church. It is, therefore, vital that pastors form a relationship with people within their own congregation where, speaking the truth in love, they can receive honest, godly feedback and be asked penetrating, personal questions. At the very least, this sort of accountability should be part of the pastor's relationship with his elders. If a pastor has elders with whom he doesn't feel comfortable relating at this level, it may be an indication that the elders in question are not actually suitable for eldership!

Beyond this kind of structured accountability, pastors also need to regard themselves as being accountable to the whole congregation. While most people in the church may not know them well enough to comment and challenge them regarding their morality or personal spirituality, *every* church member should feel comfortable to speak to pastors if they have concerns about their teaching. And pastors, themselves, must be open to this kind of scrutiny, laying aside their pride and listening to the concerns of their brothers and sisters with humble hearts.

In a previous chapter, I mentioned an incident concerning a dear friend of mine who is a mature Christian with an excellent knowledge of the Bible. At one stage, he became very concerned about a theme of teaching by his pastor, which he believed was contradictory to the New Testament. He prepared a paper outlining how this teaching and practice contradicted the New Testament, and he met with the pastor and one of the elders to share his concerns. Not only were his concerns not listened to, and his paper largely unread, but he has now been labelled a trouble-maker. He was accused of not supporting the minister as "God's anointed leader". Sadly, this is not an isolated incident. I heard of a similar encounter recently, where the questioner was bludgeoned into silence (if not submission) with Psalm 105:15, "*Do not touch the Lord's anointed*" – a verse which has **nothing** to do with holding pastors to account for the doctrine that they preach!

Every Christian needs accountability, and pastors are not exempt. Even the great Apostle Peter was rebuked and corrected by Paul when his teaching had diverged from God's truth:

"*But when Peter came to Antioch, <u>I opposed him to his face, because he was in error</u>*" (Galatians 2:11).

If we love God's church and want to protect it from tragedy and loss of reputation, if we love one another and want to protect one another from sin and error, if we truly care about our church leaders and want to protect and enhance their ministries, then accountability is vital. Church leaders who do not embrace this kind of accountability leave themselves open to temptation, error and pride. They also miss out on the blessing that such relationships can bring in terms of refining and sharpening them as individuals and making them more effective as God's servants.

6

WOMEN IN CHURCH LEADERSHIP

No discussion of leadership within the church is complete without examining the role of women. Can a woman be in church leadership? In the past, women have been completely locked out of significant leadership and preaching. In recent years, however, the growth of gender equality within society has led to the increasing acceptance of women as elders, minsters and preachers within some branches of the Christian church. There remain, however, divergent views regarding the biblical basis for women exercising these kinds of roles.

The role of women in the church is a complex issue which continues to be hotly debated by biblical scholars and church leaders. While it is true that some participants in the debate are strongly influenced by either feminist or chauvinist philosophies, there are also many sincere Bible scholars on both sides of the debate who have arrived at their positions as a result of rigorous study of the scriptures.

In this chapter I will propose a theological stance regarding the role of women that is hermeneutically rigorous and affirms the theological inerrancy of the Bible. In so doing, I acknowledge that others within Christendom may hold a different opinion. Love and respect should prevail in discussions of this issue.

In particular, I will deal with two questions:

1. Is there any Biblical evidence for women in leadership amongst God's people?

2. How should we interpret Paul's seemingly prohibitive statements?

IS THERE ANY BIBLICAL EVIDENCE FOR WOMEN IN LEADERSHIP AMONGST GOD'S PEOPLE?

DEBORAH

The clearest example of a woman in leadership is Deborah who, in Judges 4:4, is said to have been *"leading Israel"*. The Hebrew word for *"lead"* used here is *"shaphat"* which, according to Strong's Exhaustive Concordance of The Bible, means *"to judge; to govern"*. Clearly the people perceived Deborah as their leader and God was using her in this position, for the next verse tells us: *"She held court under the Palm of Deborah between Ramah and Bethel in the hill country of*

Ephraim, and the Israelites came to her to have their disputes decided". The next verse (v.6) sees her summoning the military leader, Barak, and giving him commands. In all of this, she appears to have exercised the same kind of godly authority among the people as did Moses and the male judges of her era.

Some critics point to Deborah's song of praise in Judges 5, where, after Israel's victory in battle, she proclaimed: *"the princes of Israel take the lead"*. This, it is claimed, is an indication of Deborah's subservience to the male leaders of Israel. Two things must be said at this point:

1. The *"princes of Israel"* were a class of nobility within the nation; a wealthy aristocracy by virtue of their birth, rather than as a result of any call of God.

2. Traditionally it was these princes who captained the armed forces in battle. This was true not only in Deborah's time, but also during Moses' leadership and right throughout Israel's history.

Deborah's praise of the *"princes of Israel"* is, therefore, simply a recognition of their front position in the battle lines and does not undermines her authority as Israel's leader.

Some people point to the fact that there is no specific mention of God having appointed Deborah as leader, and suggest that she is in such a position illegitimately. It needs to be said, however, that several of the male judges are documented without any recorded call of God (Shamgar; Abimelech; Tola; Jair; Ibzan; Elon; Abdon). The omission of such a recorded call cannot be used to infer that they were not appointed by God. In fact, the whole narrative of the book of Judges clearly infers that ALL the judges were raised up and used by God. The overwhelming theme of the book is the sovereignty and compassion of God in raising up leaders to deliver the nation. Deborah is one such leader, and the fact that her narrative is one of the longest in the book shows in what high regard she was held.

PHOEBE

In Romans 16:1 Paul refers to Phoebe as a "*diakonos*". This term was used in two ways in the New Testament. Firstly, it referred to the office of deacon, whose task was to supervise and co-ordinate some of the practical and pastoral ministries of the church (Acts 6:1-7). The importance of their role is indicated by the qualifications necessary: they had to be *"full of the Spirit and wisdom"* (Acts 6:3).

The second usage of the term "*diakonos*" was as a more general reference to the ministry of God's Word. Paul regularly applied the term to himself as a minister of the true gospel (1 Corinthians 3:5; 2 Corinthians 3:6; 6:4; 11:23; Ephesians 3:7; Philippians 1:1; Colossians 1:23,25) and also used it for his colleagues in the gospel (2 Corinthians 11:23; Ephesians 6:21; Colossians 1:7; 4:7; 1 Thessalonians 3:2; 1 Timothy 4:6).

Which of these two usages Paul has in mind here is not unequivocally evident, but we have Paul's additional statement in the next verse, Romans 16:2:

"I ask you to receive her in the Lord in a way worthy of the saints and to give her any help she may need from you, for she has been a great help to many people, including me".

While this passage is not definitive, one must consider the possibility that Phoebe was engaged in some form of itinerant gospel ministry, based at Cenchrea, but involving visits to other cities. Paul is here asking for the church at Rome to support her in her forthcoming visit to them.

PRISCILLA

In Acts 18:18 we find Priscilla and Aquilla (her husband) travelling in the company of Paul, apparently sharing the gospel ministry with him. Paul left them in Ephesus (v.19) where they continued the work. In verses 24-26 Priscilla and Aquilla took Apollos (a preacher of the gospel) aside and instructed him further in the faith. Significantly Priscilla is mentioned first in these passages, before her husband, perhaps indicating that she came from a higher social status, but more likely (given the spiritual tone of the book of Acts) because she was more prominent in Christian ministry.

Critics of this view argue that Priscilla's ministry to Apollos was not teaching, but evangelism. Yet the passage clearly indicates that Apollos was already a Christian before his encounter with Priscilla and Aquilla, for they already observed of him that *"he taught about Jesus ACCURATELY"* (v.25). Others argue that Priscilla must have been under her husband's headship during their joint ministry to Apollos and perhaps didn't do any of the teaching herself. This is pure conjecture and disregards the fact that she is mentioned first, before Aquilla.

JUNIA

In Romans 16:7 Paul speaks of *"Andronicus and Junia...who are outstanding among the Apostles"*.

Junia was a female name. In fact, it was a very common female name. The male version was Junianus or Junias. While it is true that "Junias" appears in some later variant manuscripts of this passage, the Anchor Bible Dictionary points out that *"without exception, the Church Fathers in late antiquity identified Andronicus' partner in Rom 16:7 as a woman, as did minuscule 33 in the 9th century which records iounia with an acute accent. Only later medieval copyists of Rom 16:7 who could not imagine a woman being an apostle wrote the masculine name 'Junias.'"*

Some critics argue that Andronicus and Junia were not actually Apostles, but simply had an outstanding reputation among the Apostles. This, however, is not the most natural way to read the text, and certainly disregards the evidence of verse 7, which tells us that they *"have been in prison with me"*. The most natural reading of this passage is that Junia was an outstanding woman Apostle who had been imprisoned for her gospel preaching.

EUODIA AND SYNTYCHE

In Philippians 4:2-3, Paul mentions Euodia and Syntyche and describes them as his *"loyal fellow workers"* who have *"contended at my side in the cause of the gospel"*. The majority of evangelical scholars agree that this statement by Paul is best interpreted to mean that these women had actively participated in the preaching of the gospel. Paul would not have used such athletic imagery to describe their ministry had they simply been his cooks or handmaids!

Verse 1 also suggests that these two women held positions of prominence within the church at Philippi. They were apparently in disagreement, causing Paul to exhort them to *"agree with each other in the Lord"*. The fact that their dispute was public enough for Paul to have heard of it, seems to suggest that they exercised some form of teaching or leadership role within the church at Philippi.

WOMEN PROPHETS

There also existed within the New Testament church a number of women prophets (Acts 21:9; 1 Corinthians 11:5). The existence of women prophets in the New Testament church is notable, particularly in light of the significant role that prophets played prior to the completion and canonisation of the New Testament. During this period, prophets played a crucial role, being used by God to authoritatively declare his will and his words to the church. In the case of the church in Antioch, prophets were listed as part of the leadership team, through whom God directed the church to set apart Paul and Barnabas for missionary work (Acts 13:1-4).

The authoritative and revered role of prophets is further reflected by Paul in 1 Corinthians 12:29, where he expressly ranks prophets higher than teachers. In 1 Corinthians 14:31 Paul commends prophecy as the most useful of gifts and says that those who listen to it will *"learn"*, thereby inferring a teaching component to their ministry. The fact that God gifted and called women into such an authoritative prophetic role in the New Testament church adds further weight to their partnership in all aspects of Christian ministry and leadership.

CONCLUSION

All these instances - Deborah, Junia, Priscilla, Euodia, Syntyche, the women prophets in the Corinthian church, and possibly even Phoebe – are CLEAR examples of God calling women into leadership among his people. To explain away these instances as 'exceptions to the rule' or departures from God's perfect plan for his church (as I have heard them explained) imposes an interpretation on these passages that is completely arbitrary and without scriptural justification. There is simply no hint in any of these passages that these instances of women in leadership within God's church are either exceptional or less than ideal.

There remain, however, some statements by the Apostle Paul in the New Testament that appear severely prohibitive of the role of women. What are we to make of these?

That is the topic of the next chapter.

7

PAUL'S PROHIBITIONS

In the previous chapter, we noted the women mentioned in the Bible whom God called into various types of leadership amongst his people. These included Junia (a female Apostle), Deborah (who led Israel) and several women described as having a teaching ministry (Euodia, Syntyche and Priscilla). Negating these clear scriptural examples requires major hermeneutical gymnastics.

There remain, however, some statements by the Apostle Paul in the New Testament that seem severely prohibitive regarding the role of women in the church. What are we to make of these?

HOW SHOULD WE INTERPRET PAUL'S SEEMINGLY PROHIBITIVE STATEMENTS?

As we investigate several of Paul's apparently restrictive or prohibitive comments regarding the role of women, the one thing we must assert is that God is not a God of contradiction and, as a corollary, that the Bible is not a book of contradictions. The Bible will not say one thing in one place, and then something completely contradictory in another. If the Bible has already indicated numerous, clear examples of women in leadership roles among God's people, it will not elsewhere condemn such roles. Paul's seemingly prohibitive statements, therefore, must not be interpreted in a way that contradicts or undermines these clear biblical instances of women in leadership.

Is there a way of interpreting Paul's comments as something other than a universal prohibition on women leadership, which does not inflict hermeneutical violence upon the texts? I believe there is.

1 TIMOTHY 2:11-14

"A woman should learn in quietness and full submission. [12] I do not permit a woman to teach or to assume authority over a man; she must be quiet. [13] For Adam was formed first, then Eve. [14] And Adam was not the one deceived; it was the woman who was deceived and became a sinner. "

Much of the debate concerning the role of women in the church centres around this strongly worded injunction by Paul. What are we to make of it? Firstly, we must affirm that this is indeed God's Word. We cannot dismiss it, as some attempt to, as uninspired and therefore not authoritative. Secondly, it is not just teaching with authority that is prohibited (as if there can be any other form of teaching!), but any and all teaching; for "*teaching*" and "*authority*" are completely separate elements of this sentence in the Greek text. This is correctly rendered in our English translations *"teach OR have authority"* (rather than "teach *with* authority").

The first point that needs to be made is that the word "*authority*" that is used by Paul here is not one of the more common Greek words for authority (exousia, epitage, huperoche, or dunastes), but the more unusual word "*authentein*". This means to usurp authority; to domineer (in an ungodly way). It cannot, therefore, be taken to prohibit the *general* exercise of authority, but simply the *wrongful* use of authority in a manner which lords it over others.

The prohibition against a woman teaching a man, doesn't seem, initially, to lend itself to such a simple explanation. However, there is some historical information that can assist us. There is a consensus among Bible scholars that there was, at this time in Ephesus, a false teaching with a Gnostic flavour being spread throughout the church, and that much of it was being spread via the women in the church. In that culture, the uneducated women seem to have provided the social network that false teachers could use to spread their falsehoods throughout the congregation (see 1 Timothy 5:13 and 2 Timothy 3:6-7). For this reason, some biblical scholars interpret Paul's prohibition against a woman teaching a man in 1 Timothy 2:12 to be applicable only to *that* church at *that* specific time.

Paul actually provides us with his reasons for this prohibition in verses 13 and 14, and at first glance it seems to negate this "cultural" interpretation and propose a universal application:

"For Adam was formed first, then Eve. And Adam was not the one deceived; it was the woman who was deceived and became a sinner."

Many argue that Paul is proposing that the ministry subordination of women is a part of God's created order for mankind. Yet this directly contradicts the clear Biblical examples of women in authoritative ministry and leadership among God's people. Is there any other way of interpreting verses 13 and 14, which respects the inspired nature of the text and does not contradict the clear evidence of the leadership role of women elsewhere in the scriptures?

Yes, there is. The *"for"* in verse 13 can be understood either as the *reason* for the prohibition against women teaching men or as an *illustration* of it. If we take it as an illustration rather than a cause, Paul could simply be drawing an analogy rather than making a universal statement.

Paul refers to two important facts in the creation narrative: that Eve was created second, and that she was the one deceived, not Adam. Paul's argument here could well be that he intends to connect these two facts: that she was not present when God gave the original commandment and was therefore dependent on Adam for the teaching. In other words, she was inadequately educated - like the women in Ephesus - and more likely to be led astray. This kind of analogy is not uncommon in Paul's writings. For instance, in 2 Corinthians 11:3, he uses this same story of Eve's deception by the serpent as an *illustration* of the gullibility of the whole church at Corinth (not as a *cause* of their gullibility).

This interpretation of verses 13 and 14 still supports the inspired nature of the text, is consistent with Paul's style elsewhere, and fits with the events in the church at Ephesus at the time of writing. It also provides an interpretation which does not contradict the evidence of women in teaching roles elsewhere in scripture. We must always interpret scripture with scripture. To interpret this passage as being a universal prohibition would be to directly contradict the clear Biblical examples elsewhere of women in teaching and leadership ministry.

1 CORINTHIANS 14:34-35

"As in all the congregations of the saints, women should remain silent in the churches. They are not allowed to speak, but must be in submission, as the Law says. If they want to enquire about something, they should ask their own husbands at home; for it is disgraceful for a woman to speak in the church" (*1 Corinthians 14:34-35).*

Is this a universal truth for today, or an obsolete cultural practice from the 1st century? This is another hotly debated passage which continues to polarise Christian opinion. There are some historical and cultural issues, however, that we must consider as we seek to interpret this seemingly prohibitive statement by Paul.

In 1st century Jewish society, women were viewed as inferior and ignorant, and were kept that way through lack of access to education. Only boys were educated. Women were, therefore, not allowed to speak in synagogues or any other public meetings, because they were regarded as having nothing worthwhile to say: their uneducated opinions were not welcome. A woman's silence in a public meeting was also a symbol of her subservience to her husband. A woman who spoke in a public meeting was considered brazen and disrespectful; she brought disgrace upon herself and dishonour upon her husband, because she was not *"in submission"* to him (v34).

Paul is referring to these entrenched cultural standards when he says, *"it is a disgraceful thing for a woman to speak in the church"* (*1 Corinthians 14:35*). By insisting on the silence of women in church he is demanding that Christian gatherings conform to accepted societal conventions. He is calling for cultural congruity so that there may be no impediment to the proclamation of the gospel. For us to insist on women's silence in church today would be *incongruous* with our society and would create a cultural barrier to the proclamation of the gospel.

We must also interpret scripture with scripture. What exactly does Paul mean by saying that women should *"remain silent"* (*v.34*) and not *"speak"* (*v.35*)? Three chapters earlier, in 1 Corinthians 11, he has already indicated that women can *"pray or prophesy"* in church (v.5), which clearly involves speaking. His demand for women's silence, therefore, cannot be interpreted as a prohibition of orderly public ministry but, instead, appears to be an injunction against disorderly interjection. This interpretation is corroborated by Paul's recommendation to wives that *"if they want to enquire about something, they should ask their own husbands at home" (v.35)*. The inference seems to be that, in the church in Corinth, some unruly women were exercising their new-found freedom in Christ inappropriately, by calling out during the worship service and asking their husbands questions. It is this disruptive behaviour that Paul is prohibiting, not preaching or prophesying.

Elsewhere, Paul recognises the valuable contribution of women in public ministry: Phoebe, a deacon of the church in Cenchrea (Romans 16:1-2), Junia, a female apostle (Romans 16:7), Priscilla, Paul's co-worker in the Gospel (Romans 16:3), and Euodia and Syntyche, whom Paul described as his *"loyal fellow-workers"* who *"contended at my side in the cause of the Gospel" (Philippians 4:2-3)* – expressions recognised by most evangelical Bible scholars as referring to Gospel preaching.

Taking all of these factors into account, Paul's instructions, in 1 Corinthians 14, concerning women's silence in church appears to be:

1. A product of first century cultural standards which are now obsolete.

2. Limited to disruptive behaviour specifically, rather than to public ministry generally.

Of course, there are those who disagree with this interpretation. They view the call for women's silence in church (1 Corinthians 14:33-35) to be universally binding. Strangely, many of these same people choose to interpret everything else in chapter 14 as culturally obsolete and no longer applicable: that everyone who comes to church should be allowed to share *"a word of instruction, a revelation, a tongue or an interpretation"* [v.26]; that two or three should be allowed to speak in a tongue provided there is an interpreter [v.27]; that two or three prophets should speak [v.29]; that they should not forbid the speaking of tongues [v.39]. On what basis are these instructions discarded as culturally or theologically obsolete, yet the demand for women's silence is retained?

1 CORINTHIANS 11:2-16

"I want you to realise that the head of every man is Christ, and the head of every woman is man, and the head of Christ is God..." (v.3)

This appears to be a universal, timeless theological truth. Indeed, it is difficult to view this passage in any other way. In verses 7-10, Paul explains that man's headship over woman stems from the nature, order and mode of their creation by God in the beginning. The headship of man over woman is compared to the headship of Christ over man and of the Father over Christ. This tells us two important things:

1. It is a hierarchy of *function* not of value (the Father and Son are equally divine)

2. This headship *does* involve at least some degree of authority (the Father had clear authority over Christ (John 4:34; 6:38-39; 5:19; 11:41-42).

That authority *is* involved is seen by the statement in verses 7-10:

"A man ought not to cover his head, since he is the image and glory of God; but the woman is the glory of man. For man did not come from woman, but woman from man; neither was man created for woman, but woman for man. For this reason...a woman ought to have a sign of authority on her head".

Those who say that this is speaking of God's authority over woman and not man's, are simply ignoring the obvious meaning of the passage; for it is clearly referring to the relationship between woman and man, not woman and God.

Let us also differentiate between what is cultural and what is timeless. The cultural practice of the day was for women to cover their heads as a sign of man's authority over them. Only prostitutes and disgraceful women went out in public with their heads uncovered. Obviously, this is no longer culturally true. The authority of man over woman is a timeless theological truth, set in place at creation, the cultural expression of which, in Paul's day, was the covering of the head.

How, then, does the teaching of man's headship over woman in this passage, relate to the teaching in the rest of the Bible of the significant ministry of women in the church?

One factor to consider is that the Greek word in this passage for "*man*" can also be translated "*husband*". Similarly, the Greek word for "*woman*" can also be translated "*wife*". Thus, in this passage, the issue being discussed may not be man's generic headship over woman in the church, but a husband's headship over the wife in the home. If this is the case, then the Bible is simply urging wives not to feel that they can lord it over their husbands, even though some wives may have "greater" gifts for Christian ministry than their husbands.

Another clue to the puzzle is found in 1 Timothy 2:12, where, as we have already seen, Paul only prohibits a woman's use of domineering or usurping authority. Women can minister alongside men in any area, provided they do not seek to lord it over men. They may (and did in the Bible) minister authoritatively, providing they do not do so domineeringly.

This kind of harmonious sharing of ministry is evidenced by Priscilla and Aquilla always being mentioned as ministering together, and by Junia being mentioned alongside Andronicus as Apostles. It is even evidenced in this passage on headship, in verse 11:

"In the Lord, however, woman is not independent of man, nor is man independent of woman" (1 Corinthians 11:11)

CONCLUSION

There is strong evidence within the Bible of God gifting and calling women into teaching and leadership roles within his church. Negating or disregarding these scriptural examples requires major hermeneutical gymnastics. In the light of these clear biblical examples of women in church leadership, Paul's seemingly prohibitive injunctions cannot, therefore, be interpreted as universal, timeless prohibitions, but must be regarded as relating to particular precipitating local and cultural factors in the churches to which they were addressed.

Whenever I am asked for my view of the role of women among God's people, my answer is simple. My view of the role of women in the church is exactly the same as my view of the role of men. A person's suitability for Christian ministry – particularly any kind of teaching or leadership role – is based upon three factors: their giftedness, their character and the call of God on their life. Gender does not come into it; it is completely irrelevant. I have reached this conclusion, not because I am a thoroughly liberated, modern man, but because of my reading of God's Word. The instances of women in leadership roles among God's people, clearly recorded for us in the Bible, are too numerous and too clear for us to ignore.

8

THE IMPORTANCE OF KEEPING WATCH

Pointing out error and challenging the status quo is not viewed very positively within the modern church. We live in an era of tolerance where, even in the church, peace and harmony are valued more highly than sound doctrine. Church members who dare to speak up and question the teaching of their church or pastor are thought to have a critical spirit and are often labelled as trouble-makers.

In a previous chapter I mentioned a friend of mine who recently became very concerned about a theme of teaching and the elitist philosophy of leadership that had developed within his current church, which he believed were contradictory to the New Testament. He prepared a paper outlining how the church's current teaching and practice contradicted the New Testament, and he met with the pastor and one of the elders to share his concerns. Not only were his concerns not listened to, and his paper largely unread, but he has now been labelled as a trouble-maker. He was accused of not supporting the minister as God's anointed leader. Sadly, this is not an isolated incident. I heard of a similar encounter recently, where the questioner was bludgeoned into silence (if not submission) with Psalm 105:15, *"Do not touch the Lord's anointed"* – a verse which has **nothing** to do with holding pastors to account for the doctrine that they preach!

This kind of elitist elevation of the pastor beyond the reach of congregational accountability used to be a disease limited to Pentecostalism but has now inveigled itself within Evangelicalism. The Bible condemns this kind of ivory tower elitism and, instead, exhorts God's people to hold their teachers to account by carefully scrutinising and evaluating what is taught in our churches.

I am aware that many Christians run from conflict and will do anything to keep the peace. They are extremely reluctant to voice concerns about matters of doctrine or practice. They value harmony and peace in the church above all else. But the Bible does not teach "peace at all costs". Truth matters. And the mature Christian is, at times, called upon to speak up against misleading teaching and defend the truth. Blaise Pascal, the 17th century mathematician, theologian and philosopher, once wrote:

"It is as much a crime to disturb the peace when truth prevails as it is to keep the peace when truth is violated."

ELDERS ARE TO KEEP WATCH

According to the New Testament, the primary function of the shepherd (elder) is not to cuddle the sheep, but to keep them *safe*. The elder is to ensure that the flock are not led astray by false teaching:

"<u>Keep watch</u> over yourselves and over all the flock, among which the Holy Spirit has made you overseers, to shepherd the church of God which He purchased with His own blood. I know that after my departure savage wolves will come in among you, not sparing the flock; and from among your own selves men will arise, <u>speaking perverse things</u>, to draw away the disciples after them. (Acts 20:28-30)

When outlining the essential characteristics of a potential elder, Paul writes that:

"He <u>must</u> hold firmly to the trustworthy message as it has been taught, so that he can encourage others by <u>sound doctrine</u> and <u>refute those who oppose it</u>" (Titus 1:9).

Similarly, Paul instructs Timothy, the preaching elder at Ephesus:

"Instruct certain men <u>not to teach strange doctrines</u>" (1 Timothy 1:3).

Inherent in these and other verses is the necessity for elders to constantly scrutinise the preaching in their church and be prepared to lovingly correct, and even rebuke, false or misleading teaching when it occurs – even if that preaching comes from their pastor. **This is the biblical mandate for eldership!** Any elder who does not have the *biblical knowledge* to discern truth from error (*1 Timothy 3:2; 2 Timothy 2:24*), and the **strength of character** to defend the truth when necessary, should not be on eldership. The pastor should be regarded as a preaching elder, a member of a team, to which he is accountable. The Apostle Paul demonstrated his willingness to correct the teaching of a fellow elder when he confronted the Apostle Peter about his wrong teaching:

"But when Peter came to Antioch, <u>I opposed him to his face, because he was in error</u>" (Galatians 2:11).

Guarding the flock from false doctrine is the elder's primary calling. In fact, it is the role to which God will hold each elder ultimately accountable. This is evident in Paul's charge to Timothy, the preaching pastor/elder at Ephesus:

"I solemnly charge you in the presence of God and of Christ Jesus, who is to judge the living and the dead, and by His appearing and His kingdom: preach the word; be ready in season and out of season; <u>reprove, rebuke</u>, exhort, with great patience and instruction. For the time will come when <u>they will not endure sound doctrine</u>; but wanting to have their ears tickled, they will accumulate for themselves teachers in accordance to their own desires" (2 Timothy 4:1-3)

Sadly, we do not see this kind of doctrinal alertness and strength of character in many elderships today. Many elders are not even aware that this is their primary responsibility. They are often elected because of their caring hearts and their loyalty to the pastor. In fact, pastors tend to nominate elders who are already "on their side" and who will support them unquestioningly. Consequently, many elderships see their primary role as supporting and protecting the pastor, rather than as guarding God's flock.

What kind of eldership do you have in your church? Are they men and women with a thorough knowledge of the Bible and a firm grasp of theological truth? Do they operate on a level of equal accountability and authority with your paid pastor? Do they watch over the teaching of your church? Do they have the strength of character to speak up and correct teaching when it errs? Do they work alongside your paid pastor in planning and formulating the teaching program of the church? These are not my own obscure ideas; this is the New Testament model of church leadership. It is a collaborative model of leadership; a team of equals who hold each other accountable and who, together, sit under the ultimate authority of God and His Word. It is a very different model to the modern infatuation with visionary, entrepreneurial professionals who are effectively distanced from any meaningful accountability and collaboration.

WE MUST ALL KEEP WATCH

The Bible is also very clear that *every Christian* has a responsibility to stand up for the truth and speak out against error – not just elders. Jesus said, *"Watch out that no one deceives you" (Matthew 24:4)*. Similarly, John writes to ordinary Christians, *"Many deceivers have gone out into the world ... watch out ... If anyone comes to you and teaches false doctrine do not welcome them into your home" (2 John 7-10)*.

John further explains that we are to actively "test" the teachings that are presented to us, rather than passively and unquestioningly receiving them:

"Dear friends, do not believe every spirit, but <u>test the spirits</u> to see whether they are from God, because many false prophets have gone out into the world" (1 John 4:1)

Luke records that when the Apostle Paul preached in Berea, the believers did not accept his teaching unthinkingly, but continually evaluated it against the scriptures to ensure that he was speaking the truth:

"Now the Bereans were of more noble character than the Thessalonians, for they received the message with great eagerness and <u>examined the Scriptures every day to see if what Paul said was true</u>" (Acts 17:11)

The Bible calls us all to emulate the Bereans. We are not meant to passively and unthinkingly accept everything that is preached in our church. Preachers are not infallible; they may sometimes err. The mature Christian is one who listens with an **open Bible** and a ***discerning mind***. We are called to test everything against God's Word, not in order to catch our pastor out, but to protect ourselves and our church from drifting into error.

Part of our responsibility to protect ourselves and our churches involves a willingness to speak out when something is taught that is contrary to, or out of balance with, the emphasis of the scriptures. This should not be regarded as a negative activity. Rather, it is an act of love. Bible commentator, Charles Simeon, comments, *"To warn people of their error is the kindest office of love"*.

Obviously, to question the teaching of a preacher can seem a daunting and intimidating task. For the preacher, too, it can be a challenging encounter. But if a preacher is a humble man or woman of God, and his or her heart's desire is to faithfully proclaim God's Word, he or she should be willing to listen to, and consider, any critique from brothers and sisters in the Lord. In fact, a preacher's true godliness (or lack thereof) will be evident by their response to this kind of critique. A preacher who refuses to seriously consider biblically-based concerns, who acts defensively, who impugns the character of the questioner and who insists on unthinking allegiance to himself or herself as God's anointed, should cause serious questions to be raised about his or her integrity and his or her true motivations.

9

OVERSIGHT OF WORSHIP

One area of oversight of the church's teaching that is often overlooked is the teaching that occurs through worship. Long before the preacher stands to give the sermon, a significant amount of teaching has already taken place in the service via the lyrics of the worship songs that have been sung. In fact, in many churches more time is spent singing than listening to the message or sermon.

The impact of worship lyrics in the formulation of people's theology cannot be underestimated. Reading and singing any kind of words aloud has a powerful effect in laying down memory patterns within the brain. Scientific research has consistently revealed that reading and speaking words aloud results in a retention rate of information and concepts that is up to 300% more effective than mere passive listening. Furthermore, when music is added to the equation, particularly music that is emotionally moving and powerful, learning and retention rates go through the roof. You only have to look at children to realise this. The quickest way to get children to learn, is to put something to music. This is why nursery rhymes are so effective. Children and adults can learn and memorise information much more efficiently when it is sung.

I believe that many Christians learn more theology through worship songs than through the sermon. The songs they sing shape their belief system in subtle yet profound ways. The words and concepts of songs embed themselves in the brain and shape the attitudes and beliefs of the worshippers long after the service is over.

If this is so, then it stands to reason that the leaders of a church ought to watch over the songs that are being sung in their church. They ought to be testing and evaluating every potential new song to assess whether it teaches the truth about God and about what it means to know him. They ought to be willing to discard or reject potential new songs if they present a message that is theologically confusing, unhelpful, contradictory or false, no matter how appealing the music may be. This ought to be a matter of the utmost importance to a church leadership team; to ensure that everything that is said and sung in their services teaches biblical truth and is helpful for building people up in the true faith.

Yet, it has been my observation that this kind of vetting and oversight of worship songs is almost entirely missing in many churches. It is as if the leadership team don't understand the powerful learning influence that songs can have. In many churches, selection of new songs is left to the worship team, many of whom have limited theological awareness. Added to this is the fact that most new songs are not written by people with theological training. The result is that songs with misleading theology can very easily slip into a church's playlist with little or no theological vetting, and those songs can significantly shape the theology of the entire congregation, at times even contradicting what is being taught in the sermon.

So, allow me to dip briefly into a theology of worship and, from there, a discussion of the kinds of songs we ought to be singing as well as the kind we ought to avoid.

A BRIEF THEOLOGY OF WORSHIP

The Bible indicates that musical worship has a two-fold purpose:

A Vertical Dimension

The first, and primary, purpose of worship in song is to glorify God by offering to him the praise that is due to his Name. This fundamental concept of worship is inherent in countless verses throughout scripture:

"All the earth bows down to you; they sing praise to you; they sing the praises of Your Name" (Psalm 66:4).

Furthermore, we are to praise God, not in the hope of getting something in return, but as a selfless expression of adoration:

"Let them praise the name of the Lord, for His Name alone is lifted up; His majesty transcends earth and heaven." (Psalm 148:13)

Indeed, this is the ultimate purpose for which mankind and the heavenly creatures were all created:

"Let all the earth praise the Lord. Hallelujah! Praise the Lord from heaven ... Praise him, all his angels!" (Psalm 148:1-2)

If the songs that we sing in our Christian gatherings do not fulfil this most fundamental of purposes, they should have no place in our meetings.

A Horizontal Dimension

Worship in song also has a secondary, horizontal purpose. We proclaim God's praises, not only to God himself, but to each other. We do this to encourage one another, to strengthen one another's faith and to remind one another of the central truths of the Gospel:

"Speak to one another with psalms, hymns and spiritual songs. Sing and make music to the Lord in your hearts." (Ephesians 5:19)

"Let the message of Christ dwell among you richly as you teach and admonish one another with all wisdom through psalms, hymns and spiritual songs, singing to God with gratitude in your hearts." (Colossians 3:16)

Significantly, both the above verses portray the dual purpose of worship in song; the vertical dimension of worshipping

God directly, and the horizontal dimension of encouraging and teaching one another. Note, also, that the teaching and encouraging of one another through worship in song is predicated upon the necessity that ***"the message of Christ dwell among you richly" (Col 3:16)***. In other words, the content of these songs, if they are to be effective in encouraging, teaching and admonishing, must be faithful expressions of the Gospel; they must reflect the true "message of Christ", not any other kind of message.

These dual purposes of worship are not separate, or mutually exclusive. We do not need two types of songs in a worship service; some that praise God and others that teach and encourage. Songs that proclaim the majesty of God and all that he has done for us through Christ are the very songs needed to teach and encourage one another. As we praise God for his greatness and thank him for our salvation, we will inevitably be strengthened and encouraged in our faith.

Inherent in this may well be an emotional response. Worship can, at times, be a deeply moving experience, but this is a by-product of worship, not the aim. We do not engage in worship in order to seek an emotional high. True worship does not have a selfish motivation. The scriptures exhort us to:

*"continually offer to God a **sacrifice** of praise, the fruit of lips that openly proclaim His Name" (Heb 13:15).*

The word "sacrifice" ("thusia") is derived from the Greek word "thuo", which means to kill or put to death. Worship, then, involves putting to death, or laying aside, our selfish desires and motivations, and rendering to God that which is due to him, purely for his pleasure, not our own. I come to a worship service seeking not to take but to give, not to receive something but to offer something. When I do this whole-heartedly, I may experience an emotional response - a lifting of my heart and an upwelling of joy – but this is not the primary purpose of worship.

ASSESSING THE LYRICAL CONTENT OF WORSHIP SONGS

Given this understanding of the dual purpose of worship songs, and taking into account the scriptural exhortation that worship should be predicated upon the fact that *"the message of Christ dwells among you richly" (Col 3:16)*, we have clear, unequivocal criteria by which we can now evaluate the lyrical content of potential worship songs. The criteria can be broken down into several key questions:

1. Do the lyrics praise God and honour His Name in a manner that is worthy of him? (Taking into account the fact that, ultimately, no words can adequately express his praise or do justice to his greatness). If a song fails this first criterion it should have no place in our gatherings. One song that particularly irks me includes the words of the chorus, *"Christ is enough for me"*. This conveys to me the concept that *"Christ is adequate for my current needs; He'll do; He'll suffice for the moment; He is the best option I've got"*. This is probably not the intent of the composer, but the lyrics leave that interpretation open. To say that I find these lyrics underwhelming and completely inadequate in expressing the supremacy of Christ is an understatement! The majesty of God, the all-knowing, all-powerful, ever-present, transcendent Creator of the universe, deserves to be praised in words that express his all-surpassing greatness, rather than words of mediocrity.

2. Do the lyrics reflect the true Gospel, the "message of Christ"? Truth is important. Lyrics that express a false gospel, a man-made gospel, are to be rejected. One disturbing trend in recent decades has been the proliferation of worship songs that centre around me and my needs – that portray Christ as the one who exists to enhance my fulfilment, rather than the Lord who is to be served and obeyed. Songs that are filled with requests to "fill me", "lift me", "move me", "draw me closer" are self-focused rather than Christ focused, expressing a desire for an experiential high or some kind of deeper spiritual fulfilment. One recent song contains the lyrics, *"I want to touch you, I want to see your face, I want to know you more"*. On the surface, this purports to be a noble spiritual sentiment, but in reality, it is a self-focused cry for a spiritual high, a kind of transcendent experience. It is also a contradiction of the scriptures which tell us that we are to "walk by faith, not by sight". The number of references to self in some songs ("I", "me", "my"), when compared to the number of references to God, reveals the disturbingly self-focused nature of some worship songs.

3. Do the lyrics confuse romantic love with devotion to God? Unfortunately, this is now endemic within evangelical Christianity. Several songs I have recently encountered include the phrase *"Jesus, I'm so in love with you"* or something similar. In a recent worship service I attended, one particularly vacuous "worship" song included endless repetitions of the bridge:

"How I love you, how I love you, how I love you, my first love

How I love you, how I love you, how I love you, my first love ..."

"*My first love*"? Really??? How completely inappropriate to use a term which is universally employed to refer to one's first romantic love - one's first experience of "falling in love" with a boyfriend or girlfriend! Significantly, the song never clearly identifies the recipient of this sentiment: God and Jesus are never mentioned. Assuming, however, that it *is* God who is being addressed, this kind of vacuous, romantic sentiment is utterly inadequate and inappropriate in addressing the all-powerful God of the universe.

As this song started to be played in a recent church service, a man nearby turned to me and said, *"Oh no! Not another 'Jesus is my boyfriend' song!"* I quietly agreed with him. Not only do songs like this represent the feminisation of worship in recent years (which leaves the average male feeling extremely uncomfortable saying they are "in love" with Jesus), but such shallow romantic sentiment is completely inadequate in expressing praise to God.

Rather than this kind of emotive, introspective drivel, the Bible exhorts us to a much more robust devotion to God that involves obedience and the submission of one's whole life to His Lordship. It is this kind of love, the love of submission, obedience and service, that needs to be expressed in our worship songs, rather than romantic sentiment.

4. Do the lyrics contain any significant content at all? A song which effectively says little more than *"I love you, I love you, I love you"* without identifying and praising any specific qualities of God is vacuous and self-focused – a euphoric wallowing in our own emotions. Chuck Colson wrote of an experience in his own church one Sunday:

"We'd been led through endless repetitions of a meaningless ditty called 'Draw Me Close to You,' which has zero theological content and could just as easily be sung in any nightclub. When I thought it was finally and mercifully over, the music leader beamed, and said, 'Let's sing that again, shall we?'. 'No!' I shouted, loudly enough to send heads all around me spinning while my wife, Patty, cringed."

5. Do the lyrics mention God at all? Surprisingly, there have been some songs written in recent years which completely fail to identify who is being praised. An example is the song mentioned above, Draw Me Close. It contains lyrics such as "Draw me close to you, never let me go", but at no point mentions God or Jesus. The "you" could be anyone – the song could easily be sung to your boyfriend or girlfriend, husband or wife. Worse, the song has zero theological content, and consists of wallowing in a desire for an intimate, emotional experience.

6. Are the lyrics understandable to most people? In order for a congregation to worship God with their minds (1 Corinthians 14:15), they must understand what they are singing. And in order for worship songs to be useful in encouraging and teaching the faith, the meaning of the lyrics must be clear. Issues that may detract from clarity include;

• Antiquated vocabulary - words that are no longer used in modern English. This can be particularly problematic with hymns written centuries ago. (e.g. The words *"deigns"* and *"repining"*, used in the first verse and chorus of the classic hymn *"Oh Rejoice Ye Christians Loudly"* would be incomprehensible to most people today).

• Technical or theological jargon (e.g. *"propitiation"* is probably not readily understood by most people)

• Awkward, inverted sentence structures in order to achieve a rhyme

• Obscure biblical allusions (e.g. *"Here I raise my Ebenezer"* in the hymn, *"Come Thou Fount Of Every Blessing"*)

• Use of obscure poetic imagery (e.g. the lyrics, *"Night with ebon pinion brooded o'er the vale"* in the hymn of the same name by Love Humphreys Jameson)

Some may argue that songs with obscure or antiquated lyrics can still be used, provided the vocabulary is explained first. But if clarity is to be guaranteed, these obscure lyrics would need to be explained ***every time*** the hymn or song is sung, for the sake of newcomers, visitors, congregants who may not have been present when it was originally explained, and even those who were present but who have forgotten. Conducting an "Olde English" vocabulary lesson each time a hymn is sung is impractical and interrupts the flow of worship. It is also unnecessary, as there are many songs written in contemporary English that can express the same concepts.

An example of a modern worship song with excellent theological content, is "Jesus Messiah":

> *He became sin, who knew no sin that we might become His righteousness, He humbled himself and carried the cross*
> *Love so amazing, love so amazing*
> *Jesus Messiah, name above all names Blessed redeemer, Emmanuel, The rescue for sinners, the ransom from Heaven, Jesus Messiah, Lord of all*

Obviously, the words "Messiah", "redeemer" and "Emmanuel" require some unpacking, but they are in a different category to antiquated English words that have fallen into disuse. These are important biblical concepts that are foundational and that church members will grow to understand more fully as they grow in discipleship. Advocating for songs without obscure lyrics is not, therefore, advocating for simplistic, superficial lyrics.

When churches evaluate worship songs for possible inclusion in their services, the first, and most important, criterion for evaluation must be their lyrical content. A beautiful melody, sweeping chord structure and a polished arrangement are not sufficient to qualify a song as worthy of inclusion. What we sing in church has a powerful, formative influence upon people's theology. A beautiful song with questionable, misleading or incomprehensible content can subtlety undermine the truth of the Gospel and lead people into beliefs and attitudes that are unhelpful and possibly harmful. Most contemporary songwriters are not theologians, and they may not have been exposed to consistently sound teaching themselves. It is, therefore, essential that pastors and elders who are responsible for the worship ministry of their church exercise wise oversight to ensure that the message of the songs does not contradict or obfuscate the *"message of Christ"* (Col 3:16).

The last three decades have seen a growing proliferation of songs which focus on articulating the self-focused emotional response of the worshipper, rather than declaring the character of God and the work of Christ. Of course, not *all* contemporary worship songs are like this; there are still some excellent Christ-focused songs being written. But too many self-focused songs are finding their way into our play lists.

The New Testament contains several examples of what are believed to be early Christian hymns, recorded for us by Paul and incorporated into the body of his letters. The publishers of most Bible translations have indicated the liturgical nature of these passages by indenting them within the text. (Look them up in your own Bible and see for yourself!) These first century hymns provide us with an excellent model of Christ-centred worship songs:

(Phil 2:6-11) "Who, being in very nature God, did not consider equality with God something to be grasped, but made himself

nothing, taking the very nature of a servant, being made in human likeness. And being found in appearance as a man, he humbled himself and became obedient to death-- even death on a cross! Therefore God exalted him to the highest place and gave him the name that is above every name, that at the name of Jesus every knee should bow, in heaven and on earth and under the earth, and every tongue confess that Jesus Christ is Lord, to the glory of God the Father."

(Col 1:15-20) "He is the image of the invisible God, the firstborn over all creation. For by him all things were created: things in heaven and on earth, visible and invisible, whether thrones or powers or rulers or authorities; all things were created by him and for him. He is before all things, and in him all things hold together. And he is the head of the body, the church; he is the beginning and the firstborn from among the dead, so that in everything he might have the supremacy. For God was pleased to have all his fullness dwell in him, and through him to reconcile to himself all things, whether things on earth or things in heaven, by making peace through his blood, shed on the cross."

These two passages of scripture (as well as Ephesians 5:19 and 1 Timothy 3:16) are examples of first century liturgical hymns, quoted by Paul in his letters. They were sung in Christian gatherings and would have been very familiar to many of Paul's readers. The difference between the lyrical content of these hymns and that of many modern self-focused hymns is stark. Significantly, there is no mention in these New Testament hymns of the worshippers being fulfilled, blessed, empowered, lifted, gifted, drawn closer, falling deeply in love or made victorious. These early Christian hymns were not about *"us"* at all. They were focused solely upon *Christ* and His saving work.

We need to formulate our model of worship from the Word of God, and not from our self-infatuated society. In particular, our worship songs are meant to celebrate the central truths of the gospel. I quoted Colossians 3:16 earlier, but let me reinforce its message again:

"Let the message of Christ dwell among you richly as you teach and admonish one another with all wisdom through psalms, hymns and spiritual songs, singing to God with gratitude in your hearts." (Colossians 3:16)

According to this verse, the act of worshipping in song is predicated upon the necessity that *"the message of Christ dwell among you richly"*. In other words, the content of these songs, if they are to be effective in praising God and teaching one another (the vertical and horizontal dimensions of worship) must be *faithful expressions of the Gospel*; they must reflect the true *"message of Christ"*, not any other kind of self-focused message.

There is certainly nothing wrong with expressing deep emotion to God in worship. **I become concerned, however, when a song is more focused on how great my love for God is, rather than on how great my God is and how great his love is for me.** Can you see the important difference of emphasis? It's all well and good to sing *"How I love you, how I love you, how I love you"* over and over again, but **why** do we love God? What attributes and actions of God evoke such love and adoration? It is those attributes and actions that deserve to be shouted aloud and sung from the rooftops, rather than our self-indulgent declarations of love by themselves. It is an interesting exercise to examine some of the songs we sing and see what percentage of a particular song is proclaiming God's greatness and all that He has done for us through Christ, compared with how much of the song is focused upon my feelings or my desire for a deeper spiritual experience.

It is my heart's desire that *"the message of Christ dwell among us richly"* in every element of the service. It is only as we lift Christ up that people will be drawn to Him in genuine faith and repentance (John 12:32). Anything that takes the focus away from Christ onto ourselves compromises the gospel and inhibits its power to bring about true conversion (Rom 1:16).

Fortunately, the last few years have seen the introduction to the Christian music industry of some contemporary songwriters have who have a strong commitment to producing God-focused, gospel-proclaiming worship songs. Emu Music, Bob Kauflin and Stuart Townend are examples of a growing number of producers and songwriters who are producing Christian worship songs with sound lyrical content. Similarly, over the same period, Hillsong have significantly improved the lyrical content of their songs. After many years of criticism from evangelical church leaders, Hillsong is now taking treating lyrical content much more seriously, and have employed a theologically trained person to vet all lyrics of new songs. Perhaps the western church has turned the corner. I sincerely hope so.

LEADERS WHO KEEP WATCH

Do the leaders of your church watch over everything that is said and sung in your services? Do they treat seriously their responsibility to *"guard the flock, of which God has made you overseers"*? If elders sit quietly in church, week by week, allowing misleading lyrics with poor theology to be sung, they are not doing their job. God calls men and women into leadership to guard the flock. That is their central calling, and one to which they will ultimately be held accountable:

"<u>Keep watch</u> over yourselves and over all the flock, among which the Holy Spirit has made you overseers, to shepherd the church of God which He purchased with His own blood. I know that after my departure savage wolves will come in among you, not sparing the flock; and from among your own selves men will arise, <u>speaking perverse things</u>, to draw away the disciples after them. (Acts 20:28-30)

"... they keep watch over you as those who must give an account" (Hebrews 13:17)

*"To the **elders** (presbyteros) among you, I appeal as a fellow **elder** and a witness of Christ's sufferings who also will share in the glory to be revealed: Be **shepherds** (poimen) of God's flock that is under your care, **overseeing** (episkopos) them—not because you must, but because you are willing, as God wants you to be; not pursuing dishonest gain, but eager to serve; <u>not lording it over</u> those entrusted to you, but being examples to the flock. And when the Chief **Shepherd** appears, you will receive the crown of glory that will never fade away." (1 Peter 5:1-4)*

10
LET'S SCRAP CHURCH VISION STATEMENTS!

If we are discussing the various strategies of modern church leadership, we can't ignore one of the most ridiculous and unhelpful strategies of the 20th and 21st centuries: the advent of church vision statements and mission statements. I have a very simple and practical suggestion: let's scrap church vision statements and mission statements altogether!

"What?", I hear you say. *"Surely not! How would we know what we are meant to do?"*

Surprisingly, the church on earth existed, and at times thrived, for thousands of years without vision statements or mission statements. Perhaps it was a fluke!

Are we really so unsure why we exist, that we need a statement on the wall to remind us? A soccer team doesn't need a vision statement. A soccer team's mission is pretty clear: win as many games as possible by scoring more goals than the opposition. Any soccer team that needs a vision / mission statement is in serious trouble! Obviously, a church is far more complex than a soccer team. Its purpose is multifaceted, its mission is complex and, I concede, congregations need to be given constant reminders, fresh insights and regular practical guidelines to equip them to fulfil the mission that God has commissioned them with. This, of course, is one of the purposes of preaching. But I question whether simplistic, cutesy vision statements and mission statements really achieve anything and, worse, whether they are actually detrimental.

HERE ARE MY CONCERNS:

1. They are based on secular business philosophies. Church vision / mission statements are an adaptation of the business strategies of the same name that swept the world in the late 80s and early 90s. Church vision and mission statements didn't arise from in-depth study of the scriptures! Nor did they come about because of divine revelation! They were introduced to church life because church leaders wanted to copy the strategic business models of successful companies and businesses in the secular world. As a result, they import a commercial way of thinking into church life. They can cause us to think of our mission in terms of hitting targets, meeting goals, making a spiritual "profit" (growth), selling a product, meeting local demand etc.

The fundament basis for vision and mission statements is

secular, rather than spiritual. Surely, I am not the only person for whom this rings alarm bells!

2. They assume that branding is necessary. In other words, vision statements and mission statements assume that it is essential for churches to decide:

"What is our particular style as a church? What is our heart? What are we going to specialise in? How are we going to differentiate ourselves from the church down the road?"

This can result in churches effectively defining themselves as, *"We are going to be a church that focuses on love"*, or *"We are going to focus on evangelism"*, or *"We are going to focus on social justice"*, or *"We are going to focus on teaching and truth"*. The problem is, I don't see the New Testament urging individual churches to specialise or to concentrate on some ministry areas at the expense of others. As far as I can discern, the New Testament urges all Christians and all churches to implement God's **whole mission** to the best of their ability. Obviously, different churches will be stronger in some areas than others, and the same church will have different strengths in different periods of its existence. This is natural. But to define one's church by intentionally articulating a specialised focus, limits its scope of reference, both now and into the future. Mark Woods, in his article in *Christianity Today*, entitled, *"Does Your Church Need A Mission Statement: Why You're Better Off Without One"*, states, *"The trouble with statements that define what you are, is that they also define what you **aren't**"*.

3. No vision / mission statement effectively encapsulates

the whole mission of God. If a church's goal is to attempt to summarise the whole mission of God in a few cute sentences, it is always going to be inadequate and possibly even misleading in its omissions. Here are some actual examples of vision statements that I have come across in different churches:

- *"Our church exists to love God and love people"*. What about evangelism? Plenty of liberal churches who negate the need for evangelism could happily adopt this vision.

- *"Proclaiming God's truth to the world"*. What about loving and caring for people? Or is this church only concerned with proclamation and didactic teaching?

- *"To make believers out of unbelievers and disciples out of believers"*. This isn't bad, but like all vision statements, its brevity leaves all sorts of omissions and misinterpretations possible. For example, what about loving people and caring compassionately for the needy, even if they aren't interested in becoming a "believer"?

The point is, God's mission for his church is too complex and multi-faceted to be condensed into a brief, pithy statement. If I am asked what would make a good vision / mission statement for a church, my response is simple: The Bible is my vision statement. The whole of God's Word is my mission statement. It took God 66 books to convey his mission to us: what makes us think we can effectively condense it to a few sentences that we can magnetise to our fridges?

4. Most vision / mission statements quickly fall into

disuse. Very quickly, no one notices them anymore. Your church vision / mission document, that took months of brainstorming and workshopping and hundreds or even thousands of person-hours and a large chunk of money to develop, now probably sits in the bottom of your drawer, seldom looked at. The harsh reality is that, in most churches, when church members are surveyed 12 months later, almost no one can recite their vision or mission statements, and those statements have made little, if any, impact on the various ministries of the church. Can you recite your vision statement? What impact has it had on your ministry area?

Churches which spend months formulating vision and mission statements can walk away from the process believing that they have achieved something of significance, when all they have done is put a bunch of words on paper; words which may even be limiting and misleading. Jesus isn't particularly concerned with what words we have typed onto a piece of paper, no matter how professionally produced the document is. He is concerned about whether we are loving, obeying and serving him in *practice*. Next time I am invited to a church meeting to formulate a new vision statement, I think I will stay home and invite my neighbour over for a meal, in the hope of sharing my faith with him.

11

CHANGING THE NARRATIVE

In preparing to write this final chapter, I spent some time researching more articles on church leadership on the internet. I used different search parameters, focusing around the term, "qualities of effective church leadership". I was disturbed to discover that almost ALL the web pages and articles that came up in the search results were discussing the qualities and characteristics of an INDIVIDUAL church leader – a paid professional – and very few discussed the concept of church leadership as a plurality. This simply reflects the modern church's infatuation with the solo, visionary leader who will take them to the promised land of church growth and success. The thinking is, *"If we can just get the right person at the top, someone with the right vision and the entrepreneurial skills to make it happen, the church will grow."*

Strangely, the church in the New Testament era experienced

explosive growth without this kind of solo professional leader! As we have seen in previous chapters, the New Testament churches all had a plurality of leaders who were mutually accountable and who led the church by means of collaboration and consensus. Although the New Testament reflects an evolving ecclesiology over a period of several decades in terms of the precise leadership structures that operated within local churches, those structures ALWAYS involved a plurality of collaborative, mutually accountable leaders. Different terms may have evolved over time to describe and define these leaders (such as shepherds, overseers, elders and pastors), yet they consistently and universally operated as collaborative teams rather than as solo performers with individual authority.

For example, in Acts 15, we find an important doctrinal decision being made, not just by Peter, and not even by the wider team of Peter and the other Apostles, but by the much larger leadership team of the Jerusalem church, consisting of *"apostles and elders"* (verse 4). Even in this early stage in the church's development, elders had been added to the leadership team in Jerusalem, to share the leadership of the church alongside the Apostles. In Luke's narrative of this event, he particularly points out that the Apostles and elders were *"of one mind"* regarding their decision (Acts 15:25), indicating that the decision was arrived at via consensus and unity. This passage is very important for our understanding of the role of professional pastors today. Even the great Apostle Peter did not have authority to unilaterally make decisions and set policy, to determine vision and implement strategies.

As the New Testament era unfolded, this model of a plurality of collaborative, mutually accountable leaders was implemented in every church throughout the known world. There were no exceptions!

Thus, in Titus 1:5, Paul reminds Titus of the crucial task that he commissioned Titus with:

"The reason I left you in Crete was that you would set in order what was unfinished and appoint elders in every town, as I directed you."

The absolute necessity for a plurality of leadership in each church was non-negotiable in Paul's mind (see also Philippians 1:1 and James 5:14).

If this is the biblical model of church leadership, how do we change the modern narrative? In many churches the model of the solo professional vision-caster and leader is so strongly entrenched, that to question it or speak against it is to place the questioner or dissenter firmly in the box of "trouble-maker". Indeed, the questioner will meet almost as much resistance from the laity as from the professional pastors in asking the church to rethink its leadership structures.

Furthermore, even in churches where a team of elders has been appointed, the way they function is often a long way from eldership as it was prescribed and practised in the New Testament. Many modern eldership teams are significantly removed from the kind of robust doctrinal oversight of the church that the New Testament indicates is their primary calling:

"<u>Keep watch</u> over yourselves and over all the flock, among which the Holy Spirit has made you overseers, to shepherd the church of God which He purchased with His own blood. I know that after my departure savage wolves will come in among you, not sparing the flock; and from among your own selves men will arise, <u>speaking perverse things,</u> to draw away the disciples after them. (Acts 20:28-30)

Furthermore, most modern elderships do not exhibit the same kind of collaborative equality and mutual accountability with the paid pastors or preachers, as was the case in the New Testament. Time and again, I have witnessed people appointed to eldership with limited theological understanding, and I have seen elderships operating more as the pastor's rubber stamp than as true leaders, called by God to shepherd his flock.

As I explained in an earlier chapter, one of the key biblical terms for elder was "poimen" (shepherd), and it is drawn directly from the fields of Israel. The two primary roles of a shepherd of a flock of sheep are to:

- Protect the flock from marauding predators

- Ensure that the flock are fed adequately, by leading them to good pasture

It is important to note again that the primary role of the shepherd is not to spend his time going from sheep to sheep, cuddling individual sheep! Have you ever seen a shepherd do that? No. The shepherd's primary job is to lead, feed and protect. The same is true in God's church. The shepherd or elder is not primarily a pastoral visitor or a counsellor, although when an individual "sheep" is in crisis the elder may be called upon to visit and pray with that sheep. But primarily, he or she is called by God to protect the church from false doctrine and to ensure that they are fed the truth of God's word. This is their primary responsibility, to which God will ultimately hold them accountable:

"... they watch over you as those who must give an account" (Hebrews 13:17)

This is the biblical role of eldership, and it is a far cry from the way many elderships operate today.

So, let me ask you again: how can we change the modern church's narrative about leadership and eldership? How can we encourage our churches to re-embrace the New Testament's model of collaborative, mutually accountable church leadership? I confess, I don't have all the answers. The New Testament model is so far removed from many of the modern church's leadership structures that nothing short of a revolution is required in some churches. It would take a bold and humble preacher or pastor to step down from his professional pedestal and embrace a team of equals who would hold him accountable. It would take a secure minister to open up his pulpit to other gifted preachers within his congregation without feeling threatened by them. This sort of change in the leadership structure of a church would also necessitate a significant re-education of the congregation who have long ago acquiesced to the business world's model of professional leadership.

I am convinced, however, that such a revolution needs to take place. Collaborative leadership among a wide team of mature equals offers protection against the imbalanced and often conflicting visions of successive senior pastors and ministers. Mutual accountability within a team of godly elders also provides greater protection against paid pastors drifting into sin or theological error. And diligent oversight of the church's entire teaching program by a team of theologically competent elders offers much greater protection against misleading or false doctrines than simply abrogating this responsibility and leaving it to the paid preacher.

Yes, a revolution is needed. But it need not be a bloody one. This book is not a call to arms – some kind of rallying cry to insurgency. No. It is a call for ordinary, Bible-believing Christians to speak out, to point their churches back to the scriptures, to dare to ask their pastors and elders to begin to operate in accordance with the clear teachings of the New Testament. It will not be easy. There is much that needs to be unlearned and discarded. It will take a secure and humble pastor to discard the presuppositions he or she has been ingrained with. And it will take a courageous church that is willing to turn against the modern tide and embrace an ancient model of leadership that has been largely forgotten. But I believe it is possible, through the power of God's Spirit.

This is a little book with big ideas. May those big ideas take root within your church and lead it health and wholeness.

ALSO BY KEVIN SIMINGTON

7 Reasons To Believe

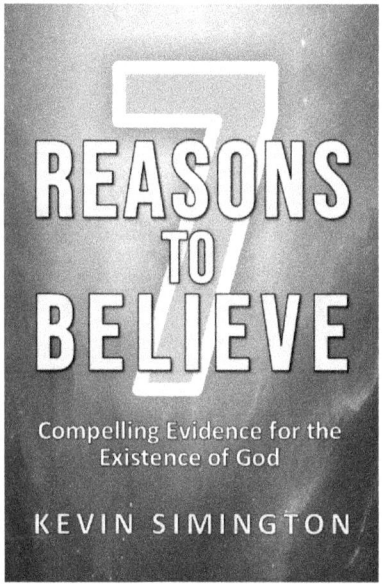

"The clearest, most up-to-date defence of the existence of God and the truth of the Christian message that I have ever read!" (Review)

7 Reasons To Believe is a clear, powerful presentation of the seven most persuasive arguments for the existence of God. Compelling evidence is examined from the fields of microbiology, genetics, cosmology, history and personal experience. Peppered with wit and brimming with meticulously-researched facts, this book will challenge even the most hardened sceptics and will strengthen the faith of those who already believe.

7 Reasons to Believe is available from SmartFaith or Amazon.

SOMEONE ELSE'S LIFE

KEVIN SIMINGTON'S NEW CRIME THRILLER!

SOMEONE ELSE'S LIFE

"A page-turning thriller by a master story-teller!"

What if you weren't who you thought you were? ... And people will kill to stop you finding out!

Much more than a simple detective story, this is a complex portrayal of a good man who is pushed to extraordinary limits.

A mysterious case of identity switching turns deadly when struggling private investigator, John Targett, becomes involved. As John seeks to unravel one mystery, he is also forced to deal with an escalating menace when he becomes the target of a vicious gang whose path he has crossed. As the twin plots intertwine and the threats escalate, John is forced to take extreme measures to protect his daughter and fight for his own life. Plagued by his own demons and trying to raise his daughter alone, this is a beautifully crafted story of the lengths to which one man will go to protect those he loves. At times tender, filled with sparkling wit and peppered with edge-of-your-seat action, this is a multi-facetted mystery that will satisfy on many levels.

REVIEW:

"An incredible thriller with the perfect twist! I adored this book. John Targett is my newest character crush! ***Someone Else's Life*** delivers on every front. It's delightful, witty, dangerous, and thought-provoking. The danger level is high throughout the novel, constantly raising the stakes and potentially making the reader breathless as events unfold. It's thrilling, and absolutely ends on the best possible note." (Kat Cohen, Reviewer.)

GET IT HERE!

THE STARPATH SERIES

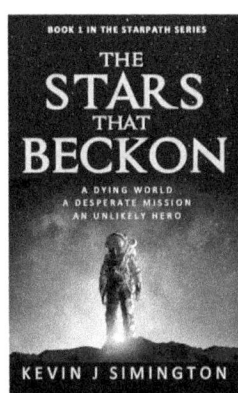  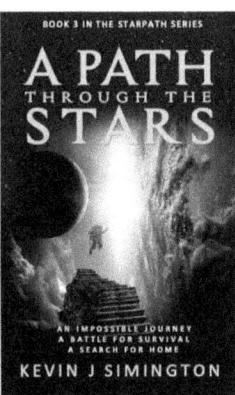

By Kevin Simington

A science fiction adventure series that is consistently receiving 5-star reviews around the world!

A dying world.

A desperate mission.

An unlikely hero.

"Incredibly well written, intelligent science fiction, by an author who really knows how to tell a story."

"I was hooked from the first page. The story is gripping and moves at a cracking pace. I also loved that there was humour and romance as well as edge-of-your-seat drama."

Book 1: THE STARS THAT BECKON

Book 2: THE STARS THAT BEND TIME

Book 3: A PATH THROUGH THE STARS

Book 4: Eden Rising

Available from Amazon

RETHINKING THE GOSPEL

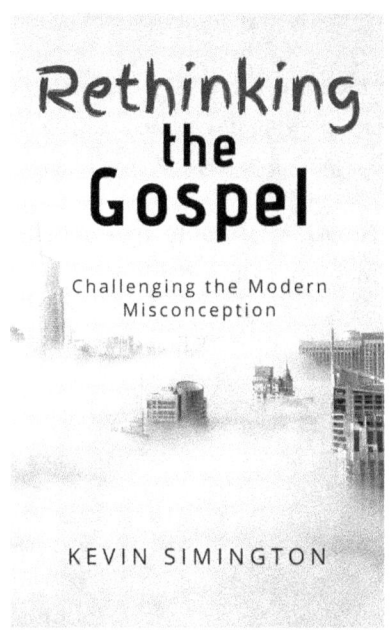

"Rethinking the Gospel" is a profoundly challenging exploration of the modern church's proclamation of the gospel. It examines an element of the gospel that has been largely ignored or under-emphasised since the start of the Reformation in the 1500's. In the modern church's rush to present salvation as a free gift, it has under-emphasised the necessity of repentance and ongoing submission to the Lordship of Christ – a theme that was a central tenet of Jesus' teaching.

"Rethinking the Gospel" will challenge you to re-examine your understanding of the gospel in the light of Jesus' consistently

confronting teaching on the relationship between faith and obedience.

One reviewer commented: *"Every church pastor, preacher and Christian should read this book! It has transformed my understanding of the gospel."*

Another reviewer commented: *"This is a devastating and eye-opening commentary on the blight that has infiltrated the modern church. It is a wake-up call that desperately needs to be heard."*

"**Rethinking the Gospel**" is available in print or as an eBook from SmartFaith.net, Amazon and all major online retailers.

MAKING SENSE OF THE BIBLE

This book will change the way you read the Bible!

"*Making Sense of the Bible*" is a comprehensive guide to understanding and interpreting the Bible. It explores the remarkable journey of the Bible, from original text to modern translation, and will assist you to develop a more mature, complex understanding of the nature of its divine inspiration. It examines the many complex cultural and contextual issues that are essential in order to accurately apply the Bible's message. These include the difference between the two covenants, the nature of progressive revelation, the pre-Christian context of the Old Testament, and the necessity to read the whole Bible "Christologically" - through the lens of Christ's person and work.

What sets "*Making Sense Of The Bible*" apart from similar books is its intensely practical nature. Commonly misinterpreted doctrines are explored in detail, and important principles of interpretation are applied. A large range of key biblical doctrines are examined in detail.

This book is a must for ordinary Bible readers and serious students alike!

"*Making sense of the Bible*" is available in print or as an eBook from SmartFaith.net, Amazon and all major online retailers.

NO MORE MONKEY BUSINESS:
EVOLUTION IN CRISIS

"*No More Monkey Business*" is a concise, easy-to-read summary of the overwhelming and rapidly accumulating scientific evidence against evolution. Written with wit, and using simple layman's language, yet brimming with incontestable scientific evidence, this book highlights the huge problems now facing Darwin's original theory. Each chapter is full of fascinating scientific facts and discoveries which now directly contradict Darwin's naïvely simplistic theory proposed more than a century ago. "*No More Monkey Business*" documents the abandonment of the theory of evolution by a growing tide of the world's leading scientists, as well as the startling declaration by several recent scientific conferences that the theory of evolution can no longer be considered to be scientifically tenable. This book will challenge those who have unthinkingly assumed evolution to be a proven fact and will enable Christians to defend their faith with confidence.

"No More Monkey Business" is available in print or as an eBook from SmartFaith.net, Amazon and all major online retailers.

FINDING GOD WHEN HE SEEMS TO BE HIDING

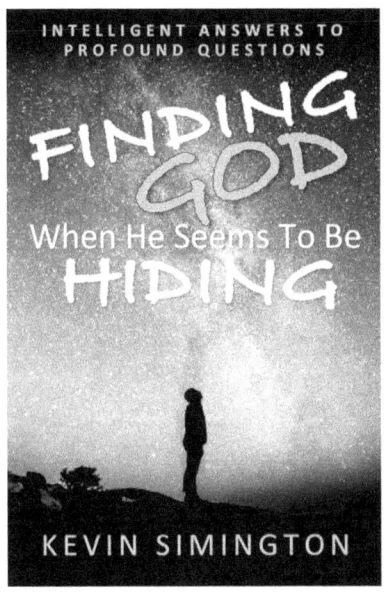

"*Finding God When He Seems to Be Hiding*" provides intelligent answers to the common questions and objections that are often roadblocks in people's journey towards faith. If God exists, why is there so much suffering in the world? What about all the killing in the Bible? How can a loving God send people to hell? Is the Bible reliable? What evidence is there for the resurrection of Jesus? What about evolution? Hasn't science and evolution disproved the existence of God? How can God permit abuse and religious violence?

This book addresses these and other common questions with

remarkable clarity and provides answers that move beyond the standard, glib responses that are often proposed.

"*Finding God When He Seems To Be Hiding*" is available in print or as an eBook from SmartFaith.net, Amazon and all major online retailers.

WELCOME TO THE UNIVERSE

"*Welcome to the Universe*" provides a fascinating glimpse into our amazing universe.

How big is our solar system? Our galaxy? The universe? Does extra-terrestrial life exist? How unique is Earth? Will we ever be able to travel to other stars? How realistic are the science fiction accounts of space travel? "*Welcome to the Universe*" addresses these and many other issues of cosmic proportion. With stunning photographs and mind-boggling facts, "*Welcome to the Universe*" provides a fascinating glimpse into the wonders of the universe and the many challenges of space travel. It is the perfect 'pocket sized' compendium for budding astronomers and armchair lovers of science and science fiction.

"*Welcome to the Universe*" is available in print or as an eBook from SmartFaith.net, Amazon and all major online retailers.

LEAVE A REVIEW

If you enjoyed this book, I would be extremely grateful if you would leave a review on Amazon, Goodreads and other review websites. Reviews are hugely important for me as a self-published author. In Amazon's case, reviews impact Amazon's algorithms, helping the book to climb higher in the charts, thereby making it more visible to potential readers. Every single review really does help!

Leaving a review is very easy. To leave a review, just go to Goodreads or the relevant Amazon page for your country, search for my book and click on the reviews link. A review of 4 or 5 stars is considered to be a positive review and a review of 3 or less stars is considered to be a negative review. (Unfortunately, Amazon only allows reviews from people who have spent at least $50 on Amazon over the preceding 12 months).

CONNECT WITH KEVIN SIMINGTON

Non-Fiction books and resources: smartfaith.net

Fiction books: kevinsimington.com

Facebook: https://www.facebook.com/ReflectionsKev/

ABOUT THE AUTHOR

Kevin Simington is a theologian and apologist who is passionate about helping Christians grow deeper in their faith. He spent 31 years in Christian ministry, as a church pastor and a Christian educator. He is now a full time author and speaker. His website, SmartFaith.net, and Facebook page, "Reflections on Faith and Life", provide valuable resources for defending the Christian faith and equipping Christians. Kevin's weekly blog, available through his website and Facebook page, provides incisive commentary on social issues, theology, apologetics and ethics, and is read by thousands of people worldwide. He also writes for "My Christian Daily", an international Christian magazine.

NOTES

www.ingramcontent.com/pod-product-compliance
Lightning Source LLC
Chambersburg PA
CBHW050318010526
44107CB00055B/2294